D1543427

Donations
courtesy
of the
Goodfellow
Coin Club

Milestone Coins

Dedicated to Bert, my wife, who has shared my interest and a fascinating journey through time with these historical treasures.

Milestone Coins

A Pageant of the World's Most Significant and Popular Money

Kenneth Bressett

www.whitmanbooks.com

MILESTONE COINS

A Pageant of the World's Most Significant and Popular Money

www.whitmanbooks.com

3101 Clairmont Road · Suite C · Atlanta GA 30329

Correspondence concerning this book may be directed to Whitman Publishing, Attn: Milestone Coins, at the address above.

ISBN: 0794823610

Printed in China

OCG™ collecting guide

Disclaimer: Expert opinion should be sought in any significant numismatic purchase. This book is presented as a numismatic history and guide only. No warranty or representation of any kind is made concerning the completeness of the information presented.

Caveat: The price estimates given are subject to variation and differences of opinion. Before making decisions to buy or sell, consult the latest information. Past performance of the rare coin market or any coin or series within that market is not necessarily an indication of future performance, as the future is unknown. Such factors as changing demand, popularity, grading interpretations, strength of the overall coin market, and economic conditions will continue to be influences.

Credits: Credit is due the following for providing images in this book: John Nebel (page 42, Eid Mar denarius); Bank Leu (page 65, Dagobert I gold tremissis); Classical Numismatic Group (page 126, German thaler); and the American Numismatic Association (page 148, $50 Assay Office gold "slug"; page 152, 1909-S VDB Lincoln cent; page 145, half dime).

About the cover, from upper left: The story of United States commemorative coins, including the popular Oregon Trail half dollar, is told on page 149. The Coventry halfpenny featuring a tower-bedecked elephant is part of the diverse variety of English Conder tokens; read about them on page 133. One of the most famous coins of antiquity is the beautiful silver dekadrachm of Syracuse, with its portrait of the water-nymph Arethusa; meet her and hear her story on pages 16 and 17. The round coin with a square hole is a Chinese "cash" coin, one of the most common pieces of money of all time; find out more on page 114. The royal lady on the Austrian thaler is Empress Maria Theresa—one of the greatest women of all time, featured on page 135. The double-daggers denarius of ancient Rome tells the tale of one of history's most famous murders; journey back in time on pages 42 and 43. The silver dollar of America's Old West was designed by an Englishman whose name would forever be attached to the coin: the Morgan dollar gets the spotlight on page 151. The small gold piece at bottom, a gold solidus of Justinian II, features the first portrait of Jesus on a coin; take a closer look on page 54. And the owl of Athens is a famous symbol from ancient Greece, one of several animals featured on coins over the centuries; learn why the bird was honored, on pages 13 and 14.

WCG™ information grid

For a complete catalog of numismatic reference books, supplies, and storage products, visit Whitman Publishing online at www.whitmanbooks.com.

Preface

Two of the most frequently asked questions about coins are "What is it?" and "What is it worth?" The questions are reasonable when someone unfamiliar with strange coins chances upon something unusual. The coins that pass from hand to hand on a daily basis become mundane, but anything that is old or odd-looking tends to conjure up thoughts that it might be rare or valuable. Sadly, the two questions that do *not* usually get asked until much later are "What is its historical significance?" and "Why was it ever used as money?"

All coins have some degree of value by their very nature. That is their intended purpose. Some are valued for their bullion content; others have an arbitrary fiat value placed on them by a governing authority. Still others are valued for their rarity and appeal to collectors. Many are seen as miniature works of art, historical documents, archaeological links to the past, or technological achievements.

Those who study and collect coins value them for all of the usual reasons as well as for the pleasure they derive from acquiring them or learning about money of the past and its economic and cultural role throughout history. Yet others view rare or unusual coins as an investment. This rather recent outlook has come about because of the increase in value of old coins brought on by a growing number of collectors. The amplified demand for certain coins has caused an increase in values because of limited supplies. There are no reserves of old coins, and would-be buyers wait for collections to again be placed on the market, and bid competitive prices to secure wanted specimens.

Beyond being sure that collectible coins are affordable, a serious numismatist does not value his or her favorite coins by their price. A $5 Indian Head cent can hold just as much interest for one collector as a $5,000 coin does for another. Value need not be measured by cost alone, but should also be discerned by the amount of information and pleasure a coin imparts to its owner. Coins, like other great works of art, should be appreciated for all their aspects of desirability.

The valuations shown in *Milestone Coins* in connection with major coin types are given as an indication of their relative current commercial worth. Many of those prices have doubled in the past five years—but that is not necessarily an indication of their investment potential. The prices of all coins are governed by supply and demand and are subject to fluctuations in economic and market conditions. Still, the steady demand for these popular coins is such that they have increased in value almost every year, and certainly have at least kept pace with all others.

Herein are my observations on what I view as some of the hobby's most popular coins. They have proven to be favorites for as long as they have been around. Among them, you are sure to find some of the pieces that you are particularly fond of and count as your personal top picks. Others may be new to you.

I invite you to explore them all, and to broaden your total enjoyment of numismatics by expanding your awareness.

Kenneth Bressett
Colorado Springs, Colorado

Kenneth E. Bressett has been involved in the hobby since the 1940s. He has written many numismatic articles and is author or editor of more than a dozen related books; a past governor, vice president, and president of the American Numismatic Association; and a highly accomplished teacher, researcher, and student. He has served for many years as the editor of *A Guide Book of United States Coins*, popularly known as the "Red Book"—at more than 21 million copies, one of the best-selling nonfiction titles of all time. As a former consultant to the United States Mint, he was instrumental in originating the 50 State Quarters® Program and in selecting many of the coins' reverse designs. Ken is a recipient of the Numismatic Literary Guild's Clemy Award and is an inductee in the Numismatic Hall of Fame (at ANA Headquarters in Colorado Springs).

Recent books by Bressett include the *Handbook of Ancient Greek and Roman Coins* (editor); the *Whitman Guide to Coin Collecting; United States Currency*; the *Official ANA Grading Standards for United States Coins* (editor); the *Handbook of United States Coins* (editor); *Money of the American Civil War*; and *Money of the Bible*.

GEORGIUS III·D·G·REX.
乾隆通寶
LIBERTY

INTRODUCTION

Milestone Coins

Introduction

People of all cultures have taken a special interest in old coins for as long as they have been around. Evidence points to the possibility that some of the original owners of ancient coins must have carefully preserved particularly beautiful examples as works of art. They likely treasured them for their aesthetic merits as well as their intrinsic value. Support for this assumption can be seen in hoard evidence, as well as in the many cases where older designs were copied and used again by later artists.

Ancient celators—skilled artisan engravers—were well aware of public interest in the quality of their engravings. A coin of superior design and technical excellence was evidence of the stability of the issuing authority. The most skillful engravers were highly sought artisans who were sometimes employed by many different cities to design their coins. Evidence points to the likelihood that roving celators not only studied but also saved examples of various coins that they wanted to emulate.

This hoard of fractional electrum pieces hails from ancient Ionia, in what is now Turkey. They are surely some of the first coins ever struck.

At a time when there were no banks, and no way to store wealth other than in the form of silver and gold coins, it was natural to select choice specimens of available pieces that could be enjoyed for the information they imparted. Caches of some diversified assortments of ancient coins tend to indicate that the earliest owners could have been collectors as well as hoarders.

Human nature has changed little over the years. Countless people have recognized the beauty and significance of coins in ways that go well beyond their monetary value. Coins are truly a reflection of history and the cultural diversification of nations around the world. Coins are the only antiquities that have survived the ravages of time and come to us—convenient and affordable—to be appreciated by all who would learn from the past.

How, other than through old coins, can anyone own a contemporary portrait of Nero, a relic of the

The owl (illustrated here on an archaic skyphos) was a familiar symbol to the ancient Greeks. This creature, sacred to the goddess Athena, traveled throughout the Greek world on the widely circulating coins of Athens.

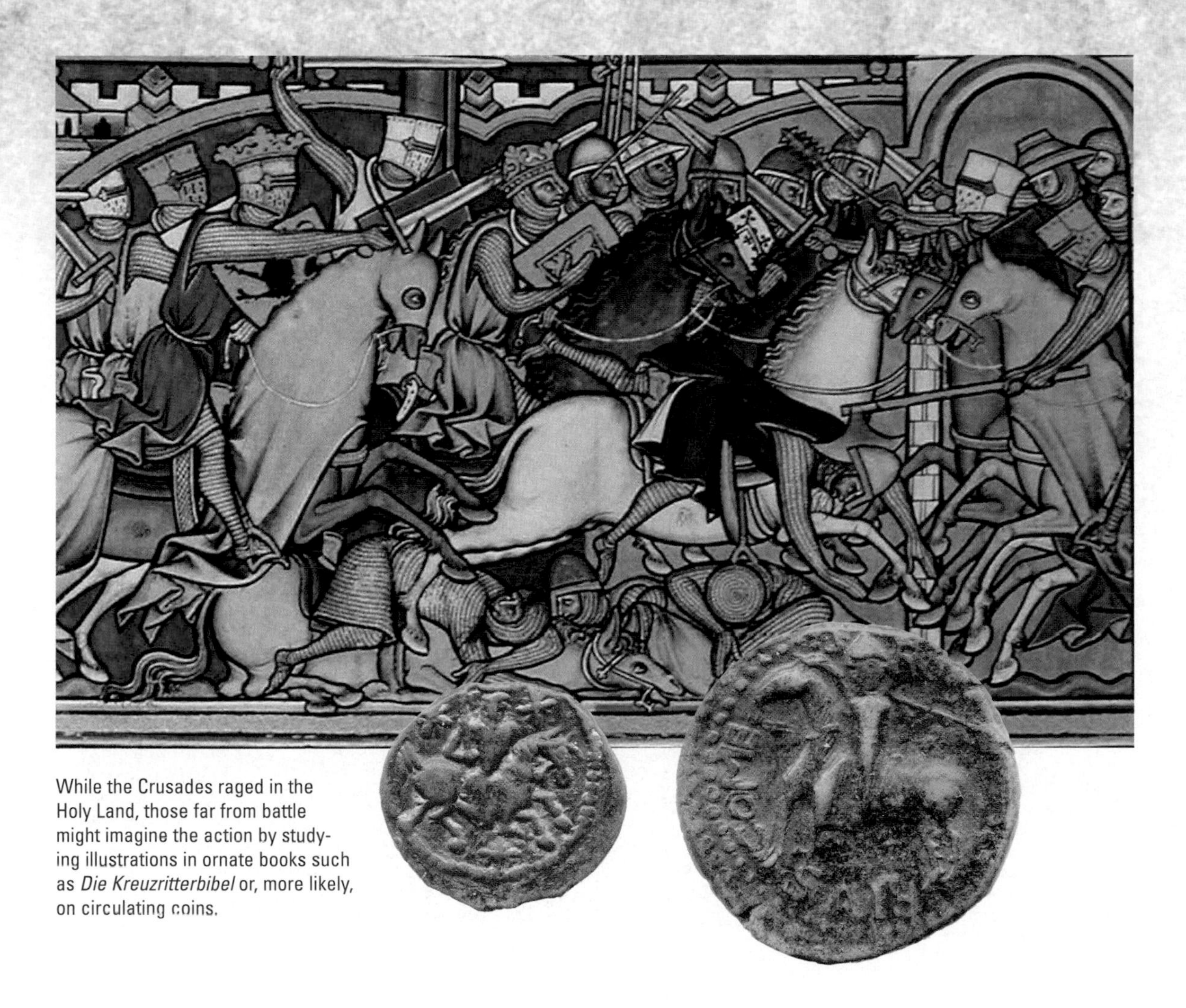

While the Crusades raged in the Holy Land, those far from battle might imagine the action by studying illustrations in ornate books such as *Die Kreuzritterbibel* or, more likely, on circulating coins.

Crusades, or a monument by Augustus Saint-Gaudens? Where, other than in great museums, can one see images of the most famous people in history and learn of the battles and tribulations associated with the beginning and end of some nations? Coins were there when history was being made, and in many instances they were part of the chronicle. It is no wonder that collectors throughout the ages have saved examples of certain coins as time capsules and reminders of the past.

George Santayana said, "Those who do not learn from history are doomed to repeat it." These words ring true when people see the world through numismatic eyes and hold in their hands tangible evidence of coins that were there when the saga of world history was unfolding. Famous tyrants, kings, saints, and heroes all have their stories recorded in metallic art. Possessing examples of these relics not only reminds us of their exploits, but it also gives us the incentive to learn more about the background of those events through books and related resources.

Consider the story of Croesus, king of Lydia in the sixth century B.C. No one was richer, and he was ruler of one of the wealthiest and most powerful nations. Concerned about Persia's rising power and weapons of destruction, he decided to make a preemptive attack. Before the conflict, he sought support from his oracles. Anxious to please their king, the oracles contrived to encourage him by pre-

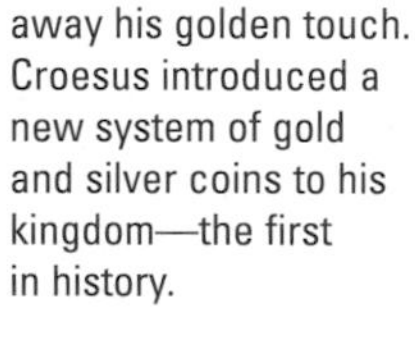

(Left) The fortune of King Croesus of Lydia, it was said, came from gold found in the River Pactolus, where the legendary King Midas had washed away his golden touch. Croesus introduced a new system of gold and silver coins to his kingdom—the first in history.

(Above) Nearly bankrupted by war in the early 1600s, and unable to muster enough silver for coins, Sweden was forced to rely on its copper mines to provide for a unique new form of coinage. The kingdom's large "plate money" weighed up to 45 pounds; the piece shown here is pictured at actual size.

dicting, ". . . if you send an army against the Persians you will destroy a great empire." Their prophecy, of course, came true, but the empire that was destroyed was not Persia, but Croesus's own. This incident comes to mind when collectors see coins of Croesus, but apparently there have been many others who have repeated his same folly in one form or another through the ages because they have forgotten this hard-learned lesson.

Another memorable message is recorded on the ancient coins of Kyrenaica, which depict the now extinct silphium plant. In earlier times silphium was considered a miracle medicine that was unsurpassed for numerous uses, with parts that were more valuable than silver. In the story of those coins, you will read what led to the destruction of every known plant and the loss to the world of an irreplaceable medication.

The stories told in this book's account of milestone coins will hopefully inspire collectors to acquire a selection of pieces that cover the span of history from 650 B.C. to the present, and discover more about the past from this process. This work is not proposed to be a comprehensive account of world coinage. The selection of pieces presented is arbitrary and only intended to represent an overview of what the author has found to be of prime interest to a majority of collectors. Experience has shown that these are some of the coins most frequently sought by collectors, and most often selected as the first to be acquired. In a sense, they are the basic cornerstone pieces that "everyone" eventually wants to own.

There is no faultless way to determine which kinds of coins are most favored among collectors. Everyone has a different idea about his or her individual preference. Certain coins seem to hold universal appeal to all collectors, and it is hoped that each of them are included in this coverage. Yet, the author recognizes that some of the pieces featured here may not be equally popular or even known to some

Through the ages, coins have celebrated rulers good and bad, whether their reigns were long and peaceful or brief and violent. King George III (far left) ruled Great Britain for more than 40 years, overseeing a dramatic, turbulent era and dying deaf, blind, and insane. Maximilian I (left and below) reigned as emperor of Mexico for barely three years, ending with a date with the firing squad.

longtime collectors. Those pieces you believe are missing will make an interesting research project for your further study.

In chronicling these coins, some attempt has been made to follow an orderly progression of coins from the oldest to the more modern issues. Samplings from each of the 10 categories are presented to show which coins have proven to be perennial favorites in each group. A collector of modern United States coins may well argue that a denarius of the Roman emperor Tiberius is nowhere nearly as popular as his 1909-S VDB cent. The ancient-coin aficionado will rebut that there is no comparison in the historic value of each. On average, both coins have proven to be well-known longtime favorites among nearly all groups of avid collectors.

Another point that will become immediately evident in this arbitrary selection of "favorites" is that they are not equally rare, expensive, or outstanding in any particular way. What they all do have in common is a background or story connected with each that appeals to all collectors. In some cases, they are rare "key" pieces needed to complete a set; others are "dream" coins that seem to elude every attempt to secure one. Some are desirable for their beauty or historical connection. Others are high on every wish list because they are things that "every collector should have." In a sense, they are all classics that seem to never go out of style.

Abraham Lincoln's portrait is the most widely circulated in coinage history, having been struck on billions of cents since 1909.

ΦΙΛΙΠΠΟΥ

CHAPTER 1

The Ancient World

The Beginning of Coinage

Ionia. Electrum 1/12 Stater. Circa 650–600 B.C.

It is difficult to imagine a time when there were no coins. The world was much different when trade and commerce had to be carried on by barter or exchange of desirable items. At that time, a measure of wheat might be traded for a weapon, or a lump of precious metal exchanged for cattle. It was an ungainly system, and with the start of commercial trading, it became necessary to find a common denominator by which goods could be valued.

A hoard of fractional gold of the era, showing various obverses and reverses.

Gold and silver were almost universally recognized as being useful and desirable. The two metals were widely accepted in trade and soon became a standard medium of exchange. In Asia Minor, transactions in the seventh century B.C. were often carried on with crude lumps of those metals that were weighed and used to pay debts. With the growth of commerce, the lumps became standardized in size and were sometimes stamped with a recognizable mark as an assurance of weight and value. The use, shape, and form were not very different from the coins we still use today.

Amazingly, some of those very first coins have survived in the sites where they were lost or buried nearly 2,600 years ago. Exactly when, where, or by whom they were made cannot be determined, but hoard evidence shows that they must have been used as money somewhere around 630 B.C. in the ancient districts of Ionia and Lydia (in what is now modern Turkey).

The earliest examples of these prototype coins were made of electrum, which is a naturally occurring mixture of gold and silver. No attempt was made to separate the two metals, and the color was usually a pale shade of yellow. The shape was globular or roughly round. Size and weight varied, and many of these early coins were no larger than the head of a nail. Despite their diminutive size, their value was probably considerable in purchasing power. The earliest coins did not attempt to include a design, but often show crude lines or anvil marks on one side and an incuse punch mark on the other.

Sometime around 600 B.C. coin makers began using simple devices on the obverse to distinguish their work. Stars, flowers, animal heads, and simply unidentifiable markings were used. On the reverses of these pieces, the mark of the rough punch that impressed the coin is always present.

Examples of the world's first coins are always popular with collectors and, happily, they are occasionally available, thanks to a modern discovery of several small pieces at the site of the temple of Artemis at Ephesus. The larger-size staters, weighing approximately 14 grams, and half staters, have always been elusive and costly.

Most of the few known examples of these coins are in Very Fine condition. Values depend on size and range from about $300 for the tiny 1/48-stater pieces, to $3,000 for the 1/3-stater coins.

8.57x actual size

A Lion in Their Midst

Lydia. Electrum 1/3 Stater. Circa 600–550 B.C.

Ancient Lydia was renowned for the wealth accessible to the area by gold bestowed upon it from nearby Mount Tmolus. The Lydians, and neighboring Ionian Greeks, were merchants well situated to carry on the commerce that flourished between the uplands of Anatolia and the sea. An account of their business enterprise was recorded by the historian Herodotus, who tells us that merchants in this region became the first shopkeepers.

Lydia's strong economy needed a convenient form of payment for their many transactions, and a means of computing sums quickly. Weighing individual nuggets of gold and electrum was time consuming and traders could not always rely on the marks of coins tested by unknown merchants. To remedy the problem, Lydian coins were marked with the lion's head that was the badge of the Mermnad dynasty—an indication of the king's assurance of honest weight and metal content.

These early Lydian coins of King Alyattes were always made of electrum, like their predecessors, and no attempt was made to manage the mixture of gold and silver, which then commanded its own price. The prevalent denomination was the 1/3-stater, or *trite*, which weighed approximately 4.7 grams. The lion design is a forceful head facing right with open mouth and standing mane. On the forehead is a radiate sun that after 2,500 years continues to defy explanation as to its meaning. The reverse shows a double incuse punch-mark.

All coins of this period were made by the simple method of striking a carefully measured lump of metal with a punch that drove the metal into a cavity that contained a design. The punch was usually square or oblong with one or two compartments. Speculation holds that only the large pieces needed to be heated before striking, and that one worker probably held the punch while another swung the mallet. A tree stump was most likely used as an anvil holder for the metal obverse die.

These attractive electrum coins of Lydia not only hold a special place in the history of numismatics, but they are also popular favorites with collectors. They are prime examples of the oldest true coins that are available from the early sixth century B.C. Whenever ancient coins are depicted or discussed in literature this is apt to be the first piece shown because of its age and bold design.

Electrum trites of Lydia can be found in various grades of condition from well worn to Extremely Fine. Values range from $800 to $1,750 for Very Fine pieces. Many show signs of ancient punch-marks that were applied to certify that some long-forgotten merchant accepted the pieces as sound. Those coins are generally valued slightly lower than unmarked coins.

Celators who engraved seal stones were employed to craft the first coinage dies. (2x actual size)

4.62x actual size

Rich as Croesus

LYDIA. SILVER SIGLOS OF CROESUS. 561–546 B.C.

The kings of Lydia controlled the mining of gold and silver and accumulated great wealth for the royal treasury in the early sixth century B.C. Their astute understanding of the needs of traders induced them to issue coins that were already weighed, guaranteed, and stamped with a royal seal of authority. The original coinage of Lydia was made of electrum found locally. Those coins were without a denomination and must have been valued according to the prevailing price of electrum.

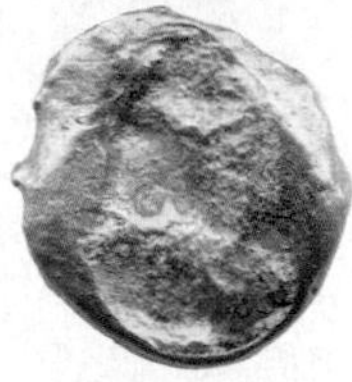

Persian gold daric and silver siglos of Darius.

Lydian kings monopolized the supply of precious metals, and thus could control market activities. Sometime around 561 B.C., King Croesus, the last and most famous Lydian monarch, abandoned the use of electrum for a dual coinage of silver and gold valued on a fixed ratio. His new coins made gold pieces 13 times more valuable than silver, and far more convenient for daily transactions. This simple fixed-ratio innovation advanced the use of coins internationally, and, until recent times, as a practice around the world.

Lydian coins are distinctive for their bold representation of the forepart of a ferocious lion attacking a bull. Both the gold and silver pieces share the same design, and can only be distinguished by their weight and color. It has been estimated that one of the gold coins was roughly equal to a month's wages. The silver coins were called *sigloi* or *shekels*.

Was King Croesus as rich as legend says? Apparently so. The ancient work *Solon* by Plutarch described him as being ". . . decked out with everything in the way of precious stones, dyed raiment, and wrought gold that men deem remarkable, or extravagant, or enviable, in order that he might present a most august and gorgeous spectacle."

History records the end of the Lydian empire as a curious quirk of fate. Croesus began to worry about the growth of power of the Persians, and conceived a preemptive battle against them. With this in mind, he consulted with oracles who convinced him of a favorable outcome of such a war. The oracles predicted ". . . if you should send an army against the Persians you will destroy a great empire." The empire that was destroyed, however, was his own, and the prophecy was fulfilled as it had been foretold.

The bimetallic system of coinage that had been so carefully devised by Croesus was taken over by the Persians when they conquered Lydia. Late in the sixth century, they too began to issue a parallel coinage of gold and silver pieces known as *darics* and *sigloi*. The Persian gold and silver coins were similar in size and weight to the Lydian pieces, but depicted a standing king with various weapons.

Specimens of Lydian sigloi are not difficult to locate and are typically included in every broad collection of ancient coins. Very Fine pieces sell for about $900. Lesser-grade pieces can sometimes be purchased for $500 to $600.

3.75x actual size

Coinage Moves to Europe

Aegina. Silver Turtle Stater. Circa 550–525 B.C.

The island of Aegina, situated off the coast of Athens, had become a central shipping depot early in the sixth century B.C. It facilitated the trade of Black Sea grain on its way to Peloponnesus, and through this exposure the merchants of Aegina became familiar with the coinage of Asia Minor. It followed naturally that Aegina would adopt its own form of coinage to further ease and promote trade. In doing so, it produced the first coins of Europe.

The people of Aegina were innovative in marking their coins with a symbol that could be easily recognized by all who saw their money. They chose the sea turtle to represent their dependence on the sea, where most inhabitants made their living. On the reverse of their coins was the imprint of the punch that forced the metal into the obverse die. The silver for their coins very likely came from the nearby island of Siphnos. Great care was taken to see that every Aegina stater was made of good silver and of full weight to ensure their acceptance in international commerce.

The reverse punch used on the earliest coins consisted of a crude eight-pronged device. Their minter's initial lack of experience seems to account for an unfortunate choice of devices and materials that frequently resulted in broken dies and imperfectly made coins. Fully struck and well-centered pieces are definitely the exception, rather than the rule. Some improvements were made around the end of the sixth century, when better-defined reverse punches were used, and again around 480 B.C. when a geometric pattern was developed. The anvil (obverse) dies underwent a similar transformation over the years, where the turtles became bolder and better detailed.

Popularity of the Aegina *chelones* (turtles) was widespread and they were eagerly accepted through the Mediterranean in the mid-sixth century. The turtles were Europe's most important trade coins until they were finally displaced by the "owls" from neighboring Athens during the fifth century, in 457 B.C. when Athens conquered Aegina and put an end to its maritime powers. This loss of Aegina's sea power seems to have been the occasion for a change in the design of their coins. The old sea turtle lost its status and was replaced by a land tortoise as the emblem of the city.

Later issues of land tortoises show a continued development in style and quality, and eventually show clearly defined shell markings and symbols in the divided punch-markings on the reverse.

Values for Aegean staters vary greatly depending not only on condition, but also to a large extent on centering and how attractive each individual coin may be. A choice Very Fine example of a turtle may sell for $1,000 or more, while a similar piece missing a part of the design, or one with a banker's test mark, might be worth only half as much. Fractional denominations exist and are quite scarce, but they are generally valued at only about half as much as the more popular staters.

Late-style coin with cross markings on reverse (top); land tortoise (middle); fractional denomination (bottom).

3x actual size

Incuse Coins of Magna Graecia

METAPONTION. SILVER NOMOS. CIRCA 530–510 B.C.

Incuse coins of Sybaris (top); Kroton (middle); and Kaulonia (bottom). (Actual size)

The first coins that were made in southern Italy are unique and original in their form. The area responsible for these very unusual coins was known as *Magna Graecia* ("Greater Greece"). The early inhabitants were transplants from Greece who settled in several distinct areas. Prominent among these colonies were Calabria, whose major city was Tarentum; Lucania, which included Metapontion, Poseidonia, and Sybaris; and to the south, Bruttium with her major cities of Kaulonia and Kroton. The distinctive feature of these coins lies in the reverse design, which is almost always an incuse (mirror image) version of the obverse.

There are no records to indicate why or how these unusual coins were made, but it is clear that they were made in those cities from around 540 B.C. until about 480 B.C. No other coinage of that period used such a sophisticated minting technique, nor is there any other contemporary coinage that approaches the artistry of these coins. Their many outstanding features of size, beauty, technology, rarity, and age place them in a unique position to be among the most desirable and popular of all ancient coins.

Legend suggests that the incuse coins of Magna Graecia should be credited to Pythagoras, the Samian philosopher and mathematician who had a reputation for being a skilled metalworker. His concept of opposite but similar designs makes this theory somewhat plausible, even though it is believed that Pythagoras might not have migrated to Italy until after the beginning of this coinage, late in the sixth century.

In physical form, these coins are impressed in relief on one side and incuse or intaglio on the other. They are struck on the Italic-Achaean standard unit of about eight grams of silver, which on the authority of Aristotle was called *nomos*, meaning "law or convention." The weights and denominations that were made for each of the colonies in southern Italy are consistently nomos, or one-third nomos. In the case of Poseidonia, half-nomos were made.

Metapontion, also called "Metapontum" by the Romans, was an ancient Achaean colony that was resettled by people from Sybaris early in the seventh century. They, and the surrounding communities, apparently agreed to use these unusual coins as a means of cooperative commerce and recognition. In doing so, they brought to the world objects of great artistry at a time when other cities were only beginning to experiment with crude coining innovations.

Many different designs were used on the incuse coins issued by southern Italian cities, and each of these designs holds a different value to collectors. The most common and well known are the barley-ear pieces from Metapontion. Early, broad examples in Very Fine condition are valued from $1,000 to $2,000; later issues on smaller, clumpy flans are priced at about half that. Related issues from other cities are usually priced much higher, sometimes up to $12,000, depending on the design, style, and condition.

2.07x actual size

Wise Old Owls of Athens

ATHENS. SILVER TETRADRACHM. 460–450 B.C.

The ancient Athenians held devotion to Athena, the goddess of wisdom, and for this they were blessed with a bountiful supply of silver from the mines at Laurium. By the middle of the sixth century B.C., rich and powerful Athenians were able to devote much of their time to cultural and aesthetic pursuits. Theirs was truly the golden age of Greece. It was during this time that their distinctive coinage began, and quickly became the most widely used and highly respected currency of the ancient world. It was a coinage that lasted unadulterated for the next 300 years.

The extensive production and wide use of Athenian silver coins made them the favorite coins of their time, and they have remained popular favorites to this day. The ubiquitous owl tetradrachms of Athens are often the first ancient coin acquired by a beginning collector, and one or more specimens are sure to be included in every collection. These coins not only hold a unique place in history, but they are also beloved for their charming design and artistry.

In the earliest beginnings of Athenian coinage, sometime around 550 to 510 B.C., a primitive style of production was employed whereby a simple punch was used to drive a blank of metal into an anvil die that held a crude design. The interpretation of the symbolism used on these early coins has eluded modern scholars. As a category, these coins are often called *Wappenmünzen*, a German word meaning "badge" or "blazon money."

By the beginning of the fifth century, coinage techniques had developed to the point where minters were then able to include comprehensive designs on both sides of their coins. Changes to the Athenian coins were made sometime before 480 B.C., when the reverse punch was replaced by a full die with the figure of an owl and the inscription ΑΘΕ. A profile head of the goddess Athena graced the obverse in a charming ensemble that could be easily understood and remembered by anyone who encountered one of these coins.

The basic Athena/owl design was continued throughout the life of this coinage with only slight modifications, part of a gradual evolution of style. The archaic fashion that permeates the entire series was an intentional feature meant to instill confidence in the public that nothing had changed in the purity and value of these coins. Their long and colorful history as the preeminent money of their time has left us with numerous anecdotes and stories about how they were used. Not the least of these is the often-used expression "Carrying owls to Athens," referring to an act of redundancy or excess.

Large and impressive tetradrachms have always been the most popular Athenian coins. They were roughly equivalent to one week's pay at that time, and probably inconvenient for all but the largest payments. To accommodate minor transactions, a full series of fractional silver pieces was produced. These included denominations down to a tiny hemitartemorion

Hemitartemorion (1/8 obol) (top); fractional denomination (middle); archaic type tetradrachm (bottom). (Actual size)

2.40x actual size

(1/8 obol) that was only slightly larger than the head of a pin. A passage from Aristophanes's play *Wasps* gives us one account of how these miniscule coins were handled in commerce, stating that it was the custom to go shopping carrying such small change in one's mouth. In retrospect, we can easily see how many of these diminutive pieces were lost over the years, and why they are so scarce 2,400 years later. The tiny Athenian owl coins are again mentioned in Aristophanes's work *The Birds*. Here he muses on the assertion of prosperity made by the Athenians:

> *Little Laureotic owlets*
> *Shall be always flocking in:*
> *You shall find them all about you,*
> *As the dainty brood increases,*
> *Building nests within your purses;*
> *Hatching little silver pieces.*

New Style tetradrachm (top); Wappenmünzen (bottom). (Actual size)

Apart from the fractional pieces, an amazing super-coin was made circa 467 to 465 B.C. It was the largest coin of the ancient world at that time, and contained 10 drachmas of silver. Why it was made is more remarkable than its size. The government was flush with wealth, so in an unprecedented move, instead of imposing an annual tax on the people, these coins were given to inhabitants of the city.

Unfortunately, such prosperity did not last forever. By the end of the long, drawn-out Peloponnesian War (around 406 B.C.), the tides of fortune had turned and Athens was reduced to issuing tetradrachms made of silver-plated copper. The exceptional emergency issue was never popular and did not last for long. Within two years the traditional silver coinage was resumed, and today only a few of the old plated coins have survived as reminders.

The Athenian experiment in issuing silver-plated emergency pieces was not the only time that the integrity of their money was put in jeopardy. Their status as international trade coins exposed them to other communities who sought to imitate the design for their own use. Some of these pieces can be distinguished by their cruder style or light weight, but many closely replicate the original Athenian pieces. The distrust brought about by the imitative coins caused numerous pieces to be tested with punch marks, or chisel cuts, to determine the internal purity of the silver.

Collectors value the ancient imitative pieces on the basis of where they were made and how closely they replicate the original Athenian coins. Pieces of only slightly cruder style are usually considered quite acceptable. Those from identifiable districts sometimes carry a premium. Obviously unsophisticated counterfeits are heavily discounted. Coins of all kinds that have heavy test cuts and punch marks are always valued lower than unmarked pieces.

The desirability and value of an Athenian coin is also influenced by its attractiveness and centering. Those displaying a full plum on Athena's helmet are the most desirable; any with part of the nose or face missing are the least valuable. Coins that were made prior to 449 B.C. are of a distinctive style that commands a substantial premium. The late-style pieces made after 393 B.C. show Athena's eye in profile, and are among the lowest-priced tetradrachms.

Sometime around 150 B.C. the so-called "New Style" coinage was introduced. These coins were struck on thinner, broader planchets; have a larger Athenian head on the obverse, with an owl perched on an amphora surrounded by a wreath; and feature magistrates' names, initials, or symbols in the field on the reverse.

Values for Athenian tetradrachms vary according to the many factors of desirability and scarcity. The "classic" pieces, those struck from about 449 to 413 B.C., are relatively common and usually available for around $400 to $600 in Very Fine condition. Earlier pieces, or those in Extremely Fine grade, may be priced up to $2,500. Late-style coins, and those with defects, are worth about half as much as the higher grades. "New Style" coins are valued about the same as the classic pieces of earlier vintage, but are somewhat less popular. • Fractional denominations are sometimes available, but most collectors prefer the tetradrachms. Small pieces generally sell for about half as much as the larger coins, but those in exceptionally high grade can bring equal prices. A few gold coins were made, but are extremely rare and costly.

Get Ready to Rumble

Aspendos. Silver Stater. 400–300 B.C.

Aspendos, in Pamphylia, on the eastern Mediterranean, was situated near the Eurymedon River and became an important port and naval base. Despite its Greek origins, Aspendos seems to have preferred Persian rule, and resisted the advances of Alexander the Great in his conquest of Asia Minor. The city issued a substantial coinage to facilitate local commerce, but their silver staters, based on the Persian weight standard of 10 grams, are considerably lighter than Attic tetradrachms of Athens and other Greek cities.

It is believed that Aspendos was founded by colonists from Argos. From the beginning of the fifth century, Aspendos and Side were the only two towns in the district to mint coins. The important river trading port was occupied by Alexander in 333 B.C. because it refused to pay tribute to the Macedonian king. It became an ally of Rome after the Battle of Sipylum in 190 B.C.

The symbolism used throughout the fourth century on most of Aspendos's coins is uniform. It consists of two wrestlers on the obverse, and usually a slinger in action on the reverse. It seems possible that these athletes were being recognized to memorialize some ancient games held in the city prior to the construction of their famous amphitheater. Just who or what sports were represented has been lost to history. The slinger may be a punning reference to the name of the city, as "Aspendos" sounds very much like the Greek word for a slinger.

Action-packed designs on the staters of Aspendos have made them popular favorites among collectors. The wrestlers are usually positioned for the beginning of a match, in Greco-Roman style, but on some coins we see other glimpses of the event, and even signs of illegal moves. The wrestlers, in traditional style, are both naked and they were most likely well greased before the match.

Staters of Aspendos are not particularly scarce, but are always elevated on collectors' want-lists because of their unusual designs. It is possible to locate high-grade pieces but expect to pay a premium because of their popularity. Worn or damaged coins are not very desirable and should be heavily discounted. The same is true of pieces that have been countermarked with bankers' punches. Some of them have three or more marks, often in the form of animals or heads.

When selecting one of these coins, collectors should strive to find specimens that please them for aesthetic reasons and fluidity of action. Sharply struck Aspendos staters are the exception, rather than the rule, but are well worth the added cost and wait in locating a desirable piece.

Action-packed designs have made these coins popular favorites among collectors.

Choice Very Fine staters of this type are usually available at prices ranging from $250 to $350. Extremely Fine coins—and those with a particularly interesting design, an exceptional strike, or fine style—can be worth double that amount or a bit more.

2.50x actual size

The World's Most Beautiful Coins

Syracuse. Silver Dekadrachm. 403–390 B.C.

Numismatists pay homage to Syracuse as the birthplace of some of the world's most beautiful coins.

The climate, location, and economic resources of Syracuse made it the jewel of the ancient world. Situated on the southeastern coast of Sicily, it was an essential port on the most important island in the Mediterranean, and for many years, the most important island in Europe. Early Greek settlers brought with them their own mythology and folklore that contributed largely to the culture, language, philosophy, and laws that shaped the foundations of Western civilization. Archimedes, the great Greek mathematician and engineer, was born in Syracuse in 287 B.C.

Numismatists pay homage to Syracuse as the birthplace of some of the world's most beautiful coins. The great celator Euainetos was active in Syracuse in the early part of the fourth century B.C., and was largely responsible for coin designs that were imitated by his disciples throughout the following century. The classic features of his portraits, and the elevated action of his racing horses, are blended into a perfectly balanced presentation. Critics from all times have agreed that the coinage designs of Syracuse are among the finest ever produced. These large silver dekadrachms (10-drachma coins) are considered to be the highpoint of numismatic art, and they have maintained a position as one of the world's masterpieces for more than 2,000 years.

The famous Euainetos dekadrachm depicts a profile head of Arethusa, nymph of springs and water, wearing a crown of leaves. She has a triple-pendant earring and necklace. Four swimming dolphins within a border of small dots surround the portrait. The inscription ΣΥΡΑΚΟΣΙΩΝ identifies this as a coin from Syracuse. Coins from dies that were personally engraved by the artist Euainetos occasionally show his name beneath the head. Those made by his apprentices can be identified by various symbols in the field.

The portrait side of these coins is considered to be the reverse because an Arethusa head had long been in that position on earlier issues. In legend, Artemis changed Arethusa into a spring of water to help her escape the river god Alpheus, and the beautiful maiden emerged on the island of Ortygia, in Syracuse, where a spring still bears her name.

What is termed the obverse of this beautiful high-relief coin depicts a charioteer driving a quadriga (four-horse chariot) and controlling the spirited team of horses by holding a kentron in his right hand and the reins in his left. Nike, flying above, is crowning the charioteer in a sign of victory. Below the ground line there is a military harness, shield, greaves, cuirass, and helmet; all of which is connected by a horizontal spear. Some specimens display the Greek word ΑΘΛΑ ("prize").

The reason for issuing these large-size coins is unclear. A prevailing theory is that they were given as prizes during the Assinarian games, first held in Syracuse in 412 B.C. If this is so, they were likely also

1.71x actual size

made, and used as prizes, for several years thereafter. The dies apparently were held in storage and reused when the need arose.

In addition to the masterful dekadrachm coins attributed to Euainetos, some equally beautiful dies were engraved by the celator Kimon. These coins were issued simultaneously with the Euainetos types from 412 to 395 B.C. The work of both of these engravers is so similar, and so beautiful, that they were both allowed to sign their dies. A unique feature of the Kimon coins is seen in his treatment of the portrait of Arethusa, and the use of a net to contain her hair.

The most prevalent coins of Syracuse were their silver tetradrachms. These too, along with several other smaller denominations, have strikingly attractive designs. Many show an archaic head of Arethusa and various displays of horses and chariots. The artistry of the coins of Syracuse changed many times over the years, but always remained in the forefront of design and execution, producing some of the world's most beautiful and enduring designs.

Collector demand for the dekadrachms of Syracuse is always high, and consequently prices are equally steep. Although specimens are occasionally available, they are not common and are always sought by museums and advanced collectors. Values are determined by many factors: condition; quality of the metal and dies; centering; and whether or not the dies were signed by the artist. Even pieces of low quality and condition command prices starting around $6,000. A choice Very Fine or Extremely Fine coin will bring up to $25,000 or $35,000, depending on its quality and individual character.

Silver tetradrachms and smaller coins of Syracuse made before and after the famous dekadrachms show many differences in style and design.

These coins have been considered masterpieces for more than 2,000 years.

Kimon-type dekadrachm. (1.76x actual size)

A Famous Olympic Winner

Macedon. Philip II. Gold Stater. 359–336 B.C.

Ask any sports fan to name one winner of the 106th Olympiad and it is a very safe bet that all you will get is a blank stare. Ask a seasoned coin collector the same question, and you will probably get the correct answer. If you are curious, it was Philip II, king of Macedon, who took the honors in 356 B.C. Not that this was his only claim to fame, but the memory of this event has been kept alive through his beautiful gold coins for the past two millennia.

Actually, the king probably did not personally participate in the horse races that he won. It was the custom at that time for a wealthy or prominent citizen to sponsor a contestant, and thus gain the honors. The relationship was similar to today's horseracing and jockey connections. Whatever the arrangement was, the king happily took credit for winning, and boldly commemorated the fact on his gold staters. The coins, which were first made around 348 B.C., depict a laureate head of Apollo on the obverse, and a galloping biga (two-horse chariot) driven by a charioteer holding a goad on the reverse.

Silver tetradrachm of Philip II. (Actual size)

Philip became king of Macedon in 359 B.C., and with his newfound power he set out to become master of the entire Greek world and whatever might lie beyond. He was especially keen to gain control of the Persian Empire, and his accomplished military skills led him close to his goal. Unfortunately, an assassin's sword cut short his grand ambition, and the undertaking was left up to his son Alexander to complete.

Gold coins of Philip II saw wide circulation. Their purity and convenient weight made them a favorite trade coin for foreign commerce. After Philip's death, the coins continued to be made without any significant change. Alexander had no desire to disrupt their acceptance, so he continued minting them with his father's name for many years.

Philip's silver coins, particularly his large tetradrachms, also alluded to the Olympic games and his love of majestic horsemanship. Some of these coins depict the king riding a pacing horse, and others show the horse with a youthful rider holding a palm branch above the horse's head. Similar designs were also used for his smaller copper coins.

Macedonian leadership throughout the fourth century B.C. had a significant influence on the entire Greek world through art and culture. Philip's coins represent a part of history that heralds the beginning of Hellenistic movement. As such, they are always popular with collectors.

Gold staters of Philip II were struck in sufficient numbers to make them still plentiful. Choice examples are priced at $2,000 to $3,000 depending on style, mint, and condition. His silver tetradrachms are still available for around $400 to $1,000, depending on grade. Copper pieces are common and may be purchased for less than $50.

3.33x actual size

Ruler of the World

MACEDON. ALEXANDER III. SILVER TETRADRACHM. 336–323 B.C.

No collection can be complete without at least one specimen of the coinage of Alexander the Great. With his unsurpassed military skill, dedication to purpose, and intelligence, he truly deserved the appellation "Great." Fortunately for all the collectors who want these coins, there are enough to go around. They were issued in such large quantities that they are still relatively common. Hoards of Alexander's silver coins are still being found at the sites of his battles or in lands where his armies traveled.

Kingship of the Macedonian Empire was thrust upon Alexander at an early age after his father's sudden death, but he lost no time in fulfilling his father's quest to conquer the Persian Empire. He then moved swiftly to extend the Greek world to the east as far as possible. His vast conquests required a prolific coinage to go with them. That was accomplished with the support of local mints that produced coins of unified designs and denominations under Alexander's direction. The number of different denominations of Alexander's coinage seems almost limitless and presents a formidable challenge to collectors.

Many of Alexander's silver coins share a uniform design: on the obverse is the head of young Heracles wearing a lion-skin, and on the reverse Zeus is seated on a throne holding an eagle and scepter. There is a long-standing speculation that the head is actually that of Alexander himself, but no firm conclusion can be drawn on the basis of his statuary. Some issues of his gold coins use the identical designs of his father, but he also issued pieces with distinctive new imagery, such as gold staters with the helmeted head of Athena on the obverse, and a standing figure of Nike holding a wreath and naval standard on the reverse. Alexander's token bronze coins usually had the head of Heracles and his symbols of club and bow.

Even after Alexander's death, coinage of the same types (and with his name) continued to be minted throughout the empire for many years. They were widely accepted and appreciated for their consistent weight and purity, and soon replaced Athenian coinage in international trade. The historical significance of these coins puts them high on the "most wanted" list for collectors of all interests. They are easily available, boldly attractive, and moderately priced.

Collectors have many choices for coins of Alexander III. The most desirable and prevalent is the silver tetradrachm. These large coins are impressive examples of Greek coinage in its heyday. A nice Very Fine example can usually be had for $250 or less. Extremely Fine pieces are $500 and up. A smaller version, the dime-sized drachma, will be priced at about half as much. Bronze coins are usually found in worn condition and are worth about $20.

The extent of Alexander's coinage seems almost limitless and presents a formidable challenge to collectors.

2.15x actual size

Queen of the Nile

Egypt. Cleopatra VII. Bronze 80 Drachma. 51–30 B.C.

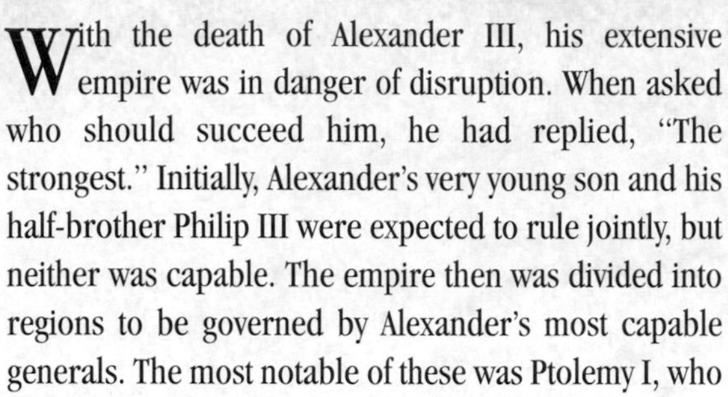

With the death of Alexander III, his extensive empire was in danger of disruption. When asked who should succeed him, he had replied, "The strongest." Initially, Alexander's very young son and his half-brother Philip III were expected to rule jointly, but neither was capable. The empire then was divided into regions to be governed by Alexander's most capable generals. The most notable of these was Ptolemy I, who was granted all of Egypt.

Silver tetradrachm of Ptolemy I. (Actual size)

The early coins of Ptolemy contained his realistic portrait and a symbolic eagle that became a standard for successive issues. There was very little innovation in Egyptian coinage throughout the entire series, which lasted until the kingdom fell to Roman rule in 30 B.C. The fundamental denominations were silver tetradrachms and didrachms, with an array of bronze token coins of various sizes from about 10 mm to 60 mm. The bronze coins were of several designs, but they all shared a version of Zeus's head on the obverse and an eagle on the reverse.

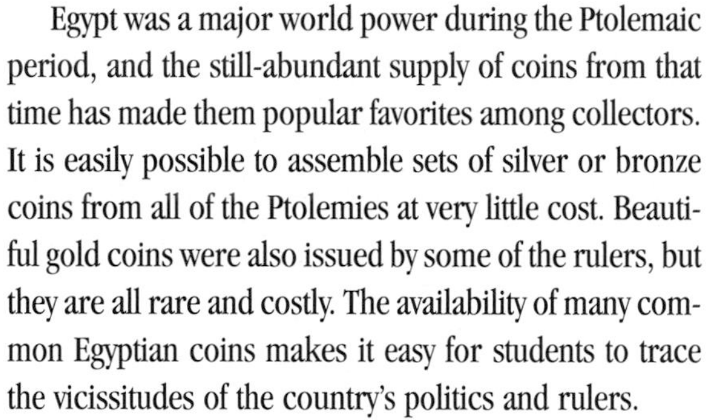

Egypt was a major world power during the Ptolemaic period, and the still-abundant supply of coins from that time has made them popular favorites among collectors. It is easily possible to assemble sets of silver or bronze coins from all of the Ptolemies at very little cost. Beautiful gold coins were also issued by some of the rulers, but they are all rare and costly. The availability of many common Egyptian coins makes it easy for students to trace the vicissitudes of the country's politics and rulers.

The early Ptolemies expanded Egypt's power through various conquests of neighboring territories, and vastly enriched the kingdom. Successive rulers wisely adopted many Egyptian customs, while at the same time encouraging the spread of Hellenism. By the end of the Ptolemaic dynasty, the rulers of Egypt were as much Egyptian in culture and philosophy as they were Macedonian in origin. The ascension of several infant kings, who ruled through their regents, contributed to political and civil strife to the detriment of the country. By the first century B.C., the former great Nile power became nothing more than a protectorate of Rome.

The most famous Egyptian ruler by far was Queen Cleopatra VII, who came to power at age 17 along with her 10-year-old brother Ptolemy XIII. The siblings ruled jointly, although as rivals, and as husband and wife, as was the custom in ancient Egypt.

Ptolemaic coins are among the most commonly available and inexpensive ancient silver tetradrachms. They have never reached their collectible potential, which is probably due to the stereotypical designs and difficulty of identification. Many Very Fine examples can be purchased for $200 to $300 each. Nice large-size bronze coins are usually priced about the same. As such, it is prudent to seek out the highest grade affordable and avoid inferior specimens. Coins of Ptolemy I, and the famous Cleopatra VII, are the most popular and always command much higher prices.

2.04x actual size

A Mystical Miracle Plant

KYRENAICA, BARKA. SILVER TETRADRACHM. CIRCA 400–331 B.C.

The coinage of Kyrenaica may seem like a strange choice for one of the *Milestone* favorites. The kingdom, and its coins, are probably unknown to most collectors, and are relatively insignificant. It is the unique plant that is shown on many of the coins from that area that qualifies these pieces for historical homage.

Kyrenaica, located in North Africa, is now known as Libya. The ancient district was also called Barka (or variously Barca, or Barke, and Kyrenaika, or Cyrenaica). It was said to be located in the eastern part of Libya, but in ancient times, Libya was all of North Africa east of Egypt, so the precise location remains unknown. The principal Greek cities in Kyrenaica were Kyrene (or Cyrene) and Barka. The region was under Ptolemaic rule in the third to second centuries B.C., when the coins under discussion were made.

Why any species of plant should deserve this kind of respect and notoriety is a story of legend, greed, and misfortune. It is a story that has been preserved in few places other than on the coins of Kyrenaica. The plant, which was known as *silphium* in ancient times, was tall and thick-stalked, with large alternating leaves and bright yellow flowers at the top. It grew particularly well in the fertile coastland between Egypt and Carthage, but apparently in very few other places. Juice extracted from the stalk and root had medicinal properties, and probably was used as a condiment. The stalk was eaten as a vegetable.

Yet, these were certainly not the only properties of the silphium plant. Its greatest appeal might have been for use in birth control, or perhaps as an antidote for poisons, or even as a hair restorer. The versatility of silphium in its many medical uses, coupled with the skills of physicians of Kyrenaica, made the district famous and wealthy.

Pliny wrote that silphium was considered to be worth its weight in silver, and described it as "one of the most precious gifts from nature to man." Apocryphal claims for the plant said that it could remove warts, preserve meat, relieve pain, put pigs to sleep, and cause carp to sneeze. It was considered poisonous to camels, but food for cattle.

The silphium plant was said to have become extinct in the first century A.D., largely due to over-harvesting, as well as resentment of the royal monopoly that controlled price, and a heavy taxation. Legend says that Kyrenaicans everywhere destroyed the plant rather than pay the tax. Today only a few relatives of the original are known to exist and we are left to wonder exactly what this miracle plant was.

Bronze coin of Kyrenaica. (Actual size)

The coins illustrated here are typical of some of the many different designs used on coins of Kyrenaica. The usual theme shows the head of Zeus-Ammon on the obverse, and the silphium plant in one form or another on the reverse. All are scarce to rare. The more common bronze pieces are worth around $100 to $200. Silver tetradrachms can be priced at $3,500 or more, with smaller denominations going for about half.

2.20x actual size

CHAPTER 2

Biblical Coins

An Ancient Day's Wages

Roman Republic. Silver Denarius. Circa 103 B.C.

Parables about coins and money are frequently used in the Bible as morality models. Those stories are well known to coin enthusiasts, and have become a canon that collectors use to identify examples of what have come to be known as "Coins of the Bible." Many ancient coins could be included in this category, but the true *Milestone* pieces are those that are specific to biblical accounts and personalities of the time.

Silver drachma of Cappadocia. (Actual size)

The Roman silver denarius is the most frequently mentioned coin in New Testament literature. It was a small coin, about the size of an American dime, and equal in size and value to a Greek drachma. Both circulated freely throughout Jerusalem at a time when there was no indigenous coinage. Either coin would have served as the customary wages for a day's pay for common laborers. In purchasing power, one silver denarius would have been equal to about $100 in today's money.

Matthew 20:1–15 specifically mentions an incident where a landowner hires laborers for his vineyard, and agrees to pay them a denarius a day. He is later accused of cheating those who worked all day, because he paid latecomers the same wages. His reply was, "Did you not agree with me for a denarius? Take your money and go."

Luke 7:41–42 tells of a certain compassionate moneylender who had two debtors; the one owed 500 denarii, the other 50. They had no means of paying so he forgave them both, and was rewarded by their love and appreciation. The incident must have been extraordinary because it would have been a rare occurrence.

Another memorable reference to these coins is detailed in the story of the Good Samaritan, as told in Luke 10:30–35. This account chronicles a traveler who on his way from Jerusalem to Jericho was attacked by robbers, who stripped and beat him, leaving him half-dead. A priest who was going the same way saw the traveler, but passed him by, and likewise a Levite saw him, but did not stop to help. Later a Samaritan approached the man, and, moved with compassion, gave him aid and brought him to an inn where he gave the innkeeper two denarii to care for the injured man.

Roman denarii were made from the time of the early Republic in 200 B.C. and were continued throughout the empire, to a point well beyond biblical days, in the second century A.D. The denarius gradually replaced the Greek drachma (which is also mentioned frequently in the Bible) as an international trade coin, and was well known through ancient times in all of the countries under Roman control.

Roman denarii were made by all of the famous Roman emperors as well as throughout the 200-year span of the Republic. As such, there are many choices to be collected as examples of coins that were talked about in the Bible. Common denarii of the Republican period are valued at about $125 for Very Fine or better specimens. Those made by emperors Augustus and Tiberius, during the lifetime of Jesus, will cost a bit more. The price for attractive pieces begins at about $225.

2.78x actual size

The Poor Widow's Mite

Judaea. Alexander Jannaeus. Bronze Lepton. Circa 100 B.C.

"Jesus sat down opposite the treasury, and observed how the crowd was putting money into the treasury; and many rich people were putting in large sums. And there came one poor widow, and she put in two mites, which make a quadran. And he called his disciples together, and said to them, 'Amen I say to you, this poor widow has put in more than all those who have been putting money into the treasury. For they all have put in out of their abundance, but she out of her want has put in all that she had—all that she had to live on.'" (Mark 12:41–44)

"Looking up he saw the rich who were putting their gifts into the treasury. And he saw also a certain poor widow putting in two mites. And he said, 'Truly I say to you, this poor widow has put in more than all.'" (Luke 21:1–4)

In these famous parables, the poor widow contributes what is described as two "mites." All accounts emphasize that the mite was the smallest bronze coin in use at that time. Although there is no actual coin known by that name, it is logical to assume that the passage refers to the very tiny bronze lepta (plural of lepton) from the time of Alexander Jannaeus, which were made by the Hasmonean head of state approximately 100 years earlier.

Lepta of Jannaeus, and other Hasmonean rulers, were the smallest and most plentiful coins of the time, and were used extensively as temple offerings during the lifetime of Jesus. It would not have been uncommon for coins a century old to continue circulating at a time when they were the only money acceptable for use in the temple. According to this parable, the two lepta were worth one Roman quadrans. There were 64 quadrans to the denarius, and thus her total offering was equivalent to 1/64 of a day's wages at that time, or approximately $1.50 in terms of purchasing power.

The story of the poor widow's mite is one of the best-known references to money in the Bible. It is no wonder that collectors and non-collectors alike avidly seek examples. Fortunately for all who appreciate these coins, they are still extremely common and readily available. Hoards of these tiny bronze pieces are constantly being unearthed in the Holy Land, and are available from many sources.

The story of the poor widow's mite is one of the best-known references to money in the Bible.

The most common Hasmonean bronze lepta are usually priced from $15 to $20 in low-grade condition. Do not expect to find Extremely Fine specimens. They are rare and may cost $100 or more when available. The majority of these coins are poorly made, off center, and well worn. Those that are sold outside of the numismatic trade, often in mass-market promotions, are apt to be barely recognizable, and priced at around $30.

4x actual size

City of the Bible

BYBLOS. KING ADRAMELEK. SILVER DISHEKEL. CIRCA 340 B.C.

Byblos is one of the oldest continuously inhabited cities. It was likely founded at least 7,000 years ago, and has contributed much to the advancement of civilization. The city is located on the coast of present-day Lebanon, north of Beirut, and originally was known as Gebal, in the general area called Canaan. Sometime after 1200 B.C., the Greeks named the coastal area Phoenicia, and they called the city *Byblos*.

Throughout the first millennium B.C., Byblos benefited from its importance as a Mediterranean trade center, and it was especially famous for its export of papyrus made from local plants. Plagued by foreign encroachments, the citizens of Byblos resisted Assyrian and Babylonian forces, but in time fell to the Persians, who held sway from 550 to 330 B.C. During the Hellenistic period that followed from 330 to 64 B.C., they adopted Greek customs and culture, but before that time they had begun their own coinage to facilitate commerce.

These coins were on the scene as biblical history was being made.

It was the scribes of Byblos who developed an alphabetic phonetic script sometime around 1200 B.C., and changed the way people have communicated ever since. They also devised a form of papyrus that was far superior to other writing materials of that time. This innovation quickly spread to Egypt and other places where books, contracts, letters, and sacred works were recorded in a manner and quantity never possible with older methods. The convenience of this paper-like material made it possible to transcribe large documents and historical records that might never have been preserved on more luxurious media such as clay, stone, metal, or hides. It was during this period that biblical accounts and ancient recollections were committed to writing.

The word *Bible* is a cognate of the name Byblos. Early Greek traders applied the name "biblos" to papyrus, and in time it came to mean "book." Eventually, it was used specifically to mean very important or religious books. From Greek, it passed to Latin, English, and other languages.

The silver dishekels of Byblos are representative of this important city and its unique contribution to recording biblical history. They were made only from about 350 to 330 B.C., and thus are relatively scarce. A smaller version, the silver 1/8 shekel, was also made at that time, and fortunately for collectors, those tiny pieces are still quite common.

The design on these coins is also of special interest to collectors. The obverse depicts a lion attacking a bull beneath an inscription in Phoenician script. On the reverse is a mythical hippocamp below a ship with warriors in full regalia. These are coins that were actually on the scene as biblical history was being made, and they played a part in supplying the papyrus upon which the first Bibles were written, as well as the city by whose name it has forever after been known.

Dishekels of Byblos are occasionally available in Very Fine to Extremely Fine condition at prices from $2,000 to $3,000. The more common 1/8-shekel coins are priced under $70.

2.15x actual size

The Gift of Hanukkah

Syria. Antiochus IV. Silver Tetradrachm. 175–164 B.C.

The Hebrew word *Hanukkah* means "dedication." It refers to an event that has been celebrated for centuries as a reminder of the rededication of the temple that had been desecrated by the Syrians in the time of Antiochus IV, the king who tried with all his might to pull Jews away from Judaism. It was his desire to assimilate them into the Greek culture of Hellenism—a move that ultimately culminated with the temple's destruction.

There is little good that can be said of Antiochus except that were it not for the stunning victory of the Jewish resistance fighters, Judaism, as it is known today, might be very different. There would be no Hanukkah festival to celebrate each year, and the numismatic world would be left without Hanukkah gelt (now, symbolic chocolate coins). The celebration is not complete without the giving of coins, and they have a deep meaning in the remembrance of events that liberated the ancient Jews from the wiles of evil Antiochus.

It was in 164 B.C., on the 25th of Kislev, that the army of the Maccabees recaptured most of Jerusalem from the Syrians and cleansed and rededicated the holy temple. A celebration followed where the spoils of war were likely distributed, with minor coins (gelt) possibly going to the children as special treats.

Closely tied to the Hanukkah celebration is the tradition of the little jar of oil that was found in the temple after it was captured. The small amount of oil it contained might have lit their lamps for only one night but it miraculously lasted for eight days and was the origin of celebrating the feast of Hanukkah for eight days. The festival, prominent after the Maccabees reclaimed the Temple of Jerusalem in 164 B.C., was called "Sukkot in Kislev" for many years, but was later changed to the "Festival of Lights," referring to the oil lamps, and later to its present name, Hanukkah.

Hanukkah is one of the few religious events with direct ties to numismatics, and it is one that can be remembered clearly through the original portrait coins of Antiochus IV, or in their modern counterparts called Hanukkah gelt. The coins of King Antiochus show his lifetime image on the obverse, and a seated figure of Zeus on the reverse. He is known to have looted the temple treasury, destroyed many holy texts, and defiled the altar by sacrificing a pig. Antiochus only succeeded in igniting the Maccabean Revolt, which ultimately granted a degree of freedom for the Jews.

Hanukkah is one of the few religious events with direct ties to numismatics.

Extremely Fine examples of tetradrachms of Antiochus IV are attractive, extremely popular, and generally available for about $500 to $600. Inferior specimens will cost less, but are apt to be unsightly, and are not recommended to the collector.

1.94x actual size

Render Unto Caesar

Rome. Emperor Tiberius. Silver Denarius. A.D. 14–37

When the Pharisees attempted to trap Jesus into betraying his allegiance either to God or to Caesar, Jesus called for a coin to show that it was issued by Caesar. It's quite likely the coin used was a silver denarius of Emperor Tiberius, who ruled from the years 14 to 27, during the lifetime of Jesus. The famous incident, and coins that were in use at that time, are some of the most favorite numismatic links to biblical history.

Jesus was posed a question that (the Pharisees thought) had no possible correct answer. A coin proved them wrong.

"Then the Pharisees went and took counsel how they might trap him in his talk. And they sent to him their disciples, saying, 'Is it lawful to pay the census tax to Caesar or not? Should we pay or should we not pay?' Knowing their hypocrisy, he said to them, 'Why are you testing me? Bring me a denarius to look at.' They brought one to him and he said to them, 'Whose image and inscription is this?' They replied to him, 'Caesar's.' So Jesus said to them, 'Repay to Caesar what belongs to Caesar and to God what belongs to God.'" (See Matthew 22:15–22. Some translations refer to a "Roman coin" or a "penny.")

The question, the answer, and the moral of this story are simple and clear. Even the coin is easy to identify because it does indeed contain the image and inscription of Caesar Tiberius. The Roman census tax was one denarius per person, or the equivalent of one day's pay. The King James Bible uses the term *penny* instead of denarius because they were approximately the same size. The census tax was also known as tribute, and throughout the years, the silver denarius of Tiberius has become widely known as the *Tribute Penny*.

As straightforward as this story seems, it has much deeper significance than is at first apparent. The Herodians who accompanied the Pharisees were there to see if Jesus would be disloyal to his obligation to pay the Roman tax. If he did, he surely would have been accused of being an enemy of Rome. The Pharisees wanted to see if Jesus would betray his Jewish allegiance. Either answer, it seemed, would alienate him to one or the other. It was a trap from which, they believed, he could not escape.

The answer that Jesus gave to his adversaries was brilliant and disarming. "Render unto Caesar the things that are his, and to God the things that are God's." That is, those who used Caesar's coins should repay him in kind, and those who asked about duty to God should be concerned with what is due to God.

Roman denarii of the emperors Augustus and Tiberius, whose coins were in circulation during the lifetime of Jesus, are common enough to be readily available, but always in high demand because of their popularity and connection with many historical events. A Tribute Penny of Tiberius in Very Fine condition will usually cost around $250. Nicer pieces might be valued up to $900, while inferior specimens can be had for as little as $100.

3.53x actual size

Moneychangers in the Temple

Judaea. Judah Aristobulus. Bronze Lepton. Circa 104 B.C.

The biblical parable about the moneychangers in the temple is well known, but what they were doing there and why Jesus drove them away is generally lost to readers. Clarification of their role in society at that time is needed to see why their conduct was considered despicable.

Judaea in the first century A.D. was under Roman rule, and out of necessity Jews were obliged to use Roman coins in everyday trade. Doing that, however, was offensive to their religious convention against the use of graven images. The old Hasmonian coins of their forefathers, with acceptable designs, had been made 50 to 100 years earlier, and even when available, they were badly worn from continual use. Yet, only authorized coins were acceptable offerings in the temple, so heathen Roman money had to be converted to something satisfactory.

In the outer courtyard of the temple were merchant's stalls where sacrificial offerings were sold to the devout. The offerings included birds and other animals, but even more important were coins. Some means was needed to exchange foreign money into the Tyrian shekels, or old copper coins of the Hasmonian princes, that were acceptable as gifts. Ultimately, the coins would be recycled and sold again by the moneychangers, who charged a fee of about 8% for their service.

The famous account is given in Matthew 21:12–13. "And Jesus entered the temple of God, and cast out all those who were selling and buying in the temple, and he overturned the tables of the moneychangers and the seats of those who sold the doves. And he said to them, 'It is written, My house shall be called a house of prayer, but you have made it a den of thieves.'"

Mosaic Law forbade charging interest on loans to fellow Jews, but the moneychangers took advantage of their unique position by adding a fee for their service. Their monopoly on items of necessity gave them an onerous advantage that was despised by all.

The Hasmonian coins that had been used at an earlier time were made to conform to Jewish restrictions on the use of a graven image. They have simple designs with only an anchor, star, cornucopia, and plain lettering. Judaean rulers from 104 to 37 B.C. issued these tiny bronze coins that were known as lepta or mites.

There are many different types and varieties of these small bronze coins. Most are relatively common and are often sold, regardless of their design differences, as "widow's mites." Fine specimens should be readily available at prices from $20 to $25.

Sacrificial offerings included birds and other animals, but even more important were coins. . . .

5x actual size

The 30 Pieces of Silver

Tyre. Silver Tetradrachm or Shekel. First Century B.C.

The famous "30 pieces of silver" were real coins—some of the most intriguing a collector can own.

One of the most compelling biblical accounts tells of the passion of Jesus of Nazareth, and how he was betrayed by Judas Iscariot for 30 pieces of silver. It is a story that is recounted every Easter, but few people realize that the "pieces of silver" are well-known ancient coins and that many examples still exist and are the prize possessions of coin collectors. For the initiated collector, these are some of the most interesting and coveted coins one can own.

Historians have determined that the coins that made up the original 30 pieces of silver were most likely tetradrachms minted in the city of Tyre in Phoenicia. They are the only logical candidates because that coin was in wide use in the district of Jerusalem at the time and was designated for use in the Jewish temple, and because the silver tetradrachm was often referred to as a "piece of silver" in ancient writings. Thirty of those coins was the price of a life at that time, as the payment for a servant accidentally killed, or the purchase of a slave.

The purchasing power of 30 tetradrachms was significant: about 120 days' pay for the average worker. The sum seems paltry for a life so dear to humanity, but it was a tempting amount for Judas, who went to the chief priests and said to them, "What will you give me if I deliver him to you?"

Fortunately for collectors, the coins of Tyre are among the most common of all large-size ancient coins. They are often readily available, but are also eagerly sought after by collectors, historians, museums, and those who have pondered the Bible's text. Many have survived because they were made and used for a very long time in and around Jerusalem.

First issued in the Phoenician city of Tyre in 126 B.C., they continued to be minted nearly every year until A.D. 69. They were very popular because of their reliable silver content and weight that was equivalent to the Jewish shekel as well as the Greek tetradrachm, making them an essential international trade coin.

The design of Tyrian shekels was never changed. They have a head of Heracles on the obverse, and on the reverse is an eagle standing on the prow of a ship. The club of Heracles is in the field as an indication that the coins were minted in Tyre. Various Greek letters on the reverse indicate the date when each piece was minted. Didrachms, or half shekels, were also minted during the same period, and with the same design. Theologically, coins with this design should not have been acceptable to the Jewish community, but out of necessity they were officially recognized and authorized for use in temple offerings.

Tyrian money was also used in the payment of Roman taxes, and might be the type of coin mentioned in another famous biblical passage that tells about finding such a coin in a fish's mouth. In Matthew 17:23–26, we read: "And when they had come to

2.07x actual size

Capharnum, those who were collecting the didrachma came to Peter and said, 'Does your master not pay the didrachma?' He said, 'Yes.' But when he had entered the house, Jesus spoke first saying, 'What does thou think, Simon? From whom do the kings of the earth receive tribute or customs; from their own sons, or from others?' And he said, 'From others.' Jesus said to him, 'The sons then are exempt. But that we may not give offense to them, go to the sea and cast a hook, and take the first fish that comes up. And opening its mouth thou will find a piece of money; take that and give it to them for me and thee.'"

The coin that was recovered would have been a tetradrachm of Tyre, equal to two didrachms—or exactly enough to pay the tax for two people. Finding such a coin in the mouth of a fish was miraculous, but perhaps not unnatural. The fish was possibly a variety of the well-known African Mouthbrooder. They have the unusual habit of holding eggs in their mouth for protection during incubation. It could have been a normal instinct for such a fish to retrieve a shiny lost coin and hold it in its mouth.

Tetradrachms of Tyre hold a prominent place in many coin collections because of their historical connection with the Bible, and especially as an example of the 30 pieces of silver paid for Jesus' life. Because of their popularity, they are always in demand and priced higher than their actual accessibility would warrant. Very Fine specimens regularly sell for $500 to $600. Well-worn pieces are sometimes offered at about $200. Didrachms are valued about the same, depending on condition.

Above: Shekel of Tyre made in Jerusalem when Jesus was about 10 years old. Below: didrachm or half shekel of Tyre. (Actual size)

> *". . . go to the sea and cast a hook, and take the first fish that comes up. And opening its mouth thou will find a piece of money. . . ."*

Parable of the Lost Coin

Syrian Silver Drachms and Roman Denarii. First Century B.C.

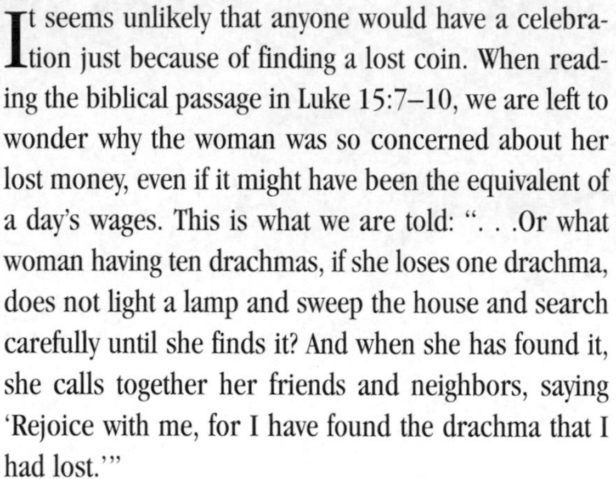

It seems unlikely that anyone would have a celebration just because of finding a lost coin. When reading the biblical passage in Luke 15:7–10, we are left to wonder why the woman was so concerned about her lost money, even if it might have been the equivalent of a day's wages. This is what we are told: ". . .Or what woman having ten drachmas, if she loses one drachma, does not light a lamp and sweep the house and search carefully until she finds it? And when she has found it, she calls together her friends and neighbors, saying 'Rejoice with me, for I have found the drachma that I had lost.'"

Anyone would be happy to recover a misplaced sum of money that was perhaps equal to $100 in purchasing power, so it is not surprising that the woman was thrilled, but why she called her friends together to rejoice needs some further explanation. The answer lies in understanding why she was so concerned with the loss.

The key to more fully appreciating this parable is in the number of coins that the woman had. The specific number of 10 drachma coins is a reference to the headband that the woman wore to signify that she was married. It would have been a symbol equal to today's wedding ring, and precious to her for many reasons beyond its monetary value.

Ten Greek drachmas were equal to 10 Roman denarii, or 10 days' pay—and a considerable amount of money. Beyond that, if a woman were found guilty of infidelity, one or more of the coins could be removed from the headband. In this story the unfortunate woman who lost one of her coins was likely embarrassed to face her neighbors and friends for fear of being accused of adultery, or as if she were in dire financial straits.

The use of drachmas and denarii on the bridal headband was an old tradition for showing status and stability. It is a custom that has been used, with some modifications, in many countries ever since. The coins were usually pierced with a nail and sewn onto a headband. No special care was taken to match the coins in any way with regard to design, age, or place of origin. It is likely that the headband coins were polished frequently, and those still in existence today are apt to be in wretched condition.

An example of one of these ancient headband coins can be an enjoyable addition to a collection of biblical coins, and an example of the stories that unusual coins can disclose. Do not expect to find one easily. Coin dealers usually do not sell common coins with holes, and many of them have been melted, buried, or lost over the years. On the positive side, when available they are sold as damaged coins, and are very inexpensive. Between $10 and $15 is about all anyone would charge; *finding* one is the challenge.

1.45x actual size

A War of Freedom

JUDAEA. SILVER SHEKEL. YEAR 2 (A.D. 67)

There was very little religious tolerance throughout the Roman Empire during the first century. Under Roman rule, colonies were allowed to practice their rites only as long as they did not disrupt or interfere with Roman policy or plans in any way. Some Roman emperors were more indulgent than others, or just too indifferent to bother with such things. Some insisted on compliance with Roman custom. One of the most infamous bigots was Nero (A.D. 54–68), who it seems held Christians, Jews, and all other sects in equal contempt.

Judaea, the home of Judaism, was under Roman control, and administered by Roman-appointed procurators between A.D. 6 and 66. During that time, there was a growing resentment of that authority and frequent rumblings about rebellion. The mistreatment and insults heaped upon the Jews by procurator Florus eventually ignited a full revolt in A.D. 66. Initial Jewish victories in routing the Roman garrisons stationed in and around Jerusalem brought a sense of liberation that inspired them to issue propaganda coins to proclaim their newfound freedom.

Rome, in retaliation, quickly took measures to ensure that the Jewish rebellion would be stamped out before it spread to other places. In Caesarea, more than 20,000 Jews were massacred in a single bloody hour. In Damascus, another 10,000 were killed. It was the beginning of a conflict that would last for the next four years, and result in the total destruction of the Holy Temple in Jerusalem and the deaths of more than 1,100,000 Jews. Still, throughout the entire war, coins were made each year to spread a message of hope to the oppressed.

The primary Jewish coins made during the First Revolt against Rome are silver shekels. Other minor bronze coins were also made, but it is the large and beautiful shekel that is so highly prized among collectors. Jewish shekels are among the most fabled and historically significant of all ancient coins and surely belong near the top of *Milestone* favorites. On the obverse of these coins are a chalice and the ancient Hebrew inscription "Shekel of Israel," with the date in Hebrew letters above the chalice. The dates refer to years one through five of the Revolt. The reverse of these handsome coins shows a stem with three pomegranates and has the inscription "Jerusalem the Holy."

In ancient biblical texts, the term *shekel* always refers to a specific weight, and not an actual denomination or coin. It was not until coins of the First Revolt were made that the Jews were able to issue their own silver coins as a mark of sovereignty. In doing so, they went a step beyond the large, thick shekel; they also made a smaller version in the weight of a half shekel of the same design.

Throughout the war, coins were made to spread a message of hope to the oppressed.

Shekels and half shekels of Israel are extremely popular, and in high demand well beyond the numismatic market. Pieces in Very Fine to Extremely Fine condition regularly sell for $1,500 to $2,500, with poorer pieces priced only slightly less.

2.30x actual size

The Bar Kochba Revolt

JUDAEA. BAR KOCHBA SILVER SELA OR SHEKEL. A.D. 132–135

Sixty-two years after the first Jewish revolt against Rome, a growing resentment was still festering. The citizens of Jerusalem longed for a messiah who would free them from the oppression of Roman rule. By A.D. 132, the situation had become intolerable, and the spark fanned into a full-blown insurrection.

The breaking point came from harassment during the rule of Roman emperor Hadrian. His grandiose plan was to rebuild Jerusalem and to rename it Aelia Capitolina. He also passed a law that forbade circumcision under the penalty of death. It was at this time that a great warrior named Simon Bar Kochba stepped forward as a leader of the resistance and the Jews' hope for a better future. The war that followed was bitter and costly, but the Jewish fighters were no match for the legions of Rome. Three years later the revolt was quelled, the city was renamed, and a temple was erected to Jupiter. Thus ended the hopes of the Jews to rebuild their dreams.

The Bar Kochba War has left us with a noteworthy numismatic legacy in the wide array of silver and bronze coins that were made during the conflict. Large silver shekels and quarter shekels were made by overstriking Jewish-inspired designs on top of existing Roman coins. These were probably made for propaganda purposes more than as functional money, and they must have been as inspiring and cherished by the people of that time as they are today. The large and very impressive shekels are key pieces in every collection, and of special interest for their unique inscriptions: "Year One of the Redemption of Israel," "Year Two of the Freedom of Israel," "For the Freedom of Jerusalem," and sometimes simply "Simon." The new, overstruck coins were also given new names to distinguish them: the Roman denarius became a *zuz* (quarter shekel), and tetradrachms were termed *selas* or shekels.

Part of the charm of these shekels comes from the design on the obverse. It is unusual in that it shows the facade of the Temple of Jerusalem in a contemporary view that is not found elsewhere. Inside the portal can be seen the Ark of the Covenant with scrolls displayed inside. On the reverse of these coins are shown the sacred *lulav* with *etrog*, used on Sukkoth, which were symbols of dedication of the temple, and associated with nature and produce.

Judaea silver zuz (top); Judaea bronze of the Second Revolt (bottom). (Actual size)

The historical connection and importance of these coins make them prime collectibles. They are showpieces and in constant demand. Shekels are the most wanted (although not necessarily the rarest) Bar Kochba coins. Nice Very Fine pieces are priced at about $2,000; some are poorly made, but few show signs of excessive circulation, so look for pieces that are at least Very Fine or better. Zuz (quarter-shekel) coins are likewise usually only available in high grade and are generally priced at $400 to $600 regardless of design or relative scarcity. Bronze coins are mostly well worn, but high-quality pieces are occasionally offered at prices that reflect their rarity.

2.20x actual size

The Spread of Christianity

Rome. Constantine the Great. Small Bronze. A.D. 307–337

Romans persisted in their dedication to ancestral deities for many decades after the rise of Christianity and its separation from Judaism. Acceptance of the new religion was not easy for the Roman hierarchy, who sometimes considered themselves divine. Yet, there were emperors as early as the third century who at least did not forcefully oppose the spread of new religious ideas.

Many late Roman coins reflect the gradual acceptance of Christianity, and one or more of these deserve to be part of the *Milestone* history of numismatics. Many collectors choose coins of Constantine I (the Great) as representative of this era. He is widely credited with being the first Christian emperor, and regardless whether this is true or not, he played an important part in the acceptance and spread of Christianity.

One of the earliest proponents of religious tolerance was Julia Maesa. She was the grandmother of Emperor Elagabalus, who ruled from 218 to 222, and was so devoted to the sun god that he tried to impose his religion on the entire empire. Through her influence, religious persecution was curtailed and a more tolerant attitude prevailed. Emperor Philip I, and his wife Oticilia Severa (A.D. 244–249), were possibly the first Roman rulers to actually adopt the Christian religion. None of these, however, was as influential as Constantine, who permitted and even encouraged conversion.

Constantine I was not the ideal Christian that one might expect. He murdered his wife and son, and although he was devoted to his mother Helena, who was a Christian, he did not convert until he was on his deathbed. Prior to that, he led a life that was anything but religious. He held allegiance to the Roman sun god, and for that reason, established Sunday as the day of worship.

Constantine intervened in ecclesiastical affairs to achieve unity. He presided over the first ecumenical council of the Church at Nicaea in 325, and he built churches in the Holy Land where his mother is credited with identifying numerous places associated with biblical events. The designs on his coins slowly eliminated references to Sol (the sun god), and those of his successors began to include religious symbols. The most prominent of these was the still familiar Chi-Rho or XP monogram, known as the *Christogram*.

Constantine I was not the ideal Christian that one might expect. . . .

Small Constantinian bronze coins of the late Roman Empire are very common and readily available. Those of Constantine the Great are the most appropriate to fill the role of this *Milestone* coin, but similar coins of his successors are equally interesting. Nice examples are always available in high grade at reasonable prices. Expect to find Extremely Fine coins priced under $50, and for those in nearly new condition the price is about double. Larger-size pieces, and those with a Christogram, will probably cost more. Dirt-encrusted pieces in poor condition are often offered at very low prices to those who want to try cleaning them.

3.33x actual size

ROMA

CHAPTER 3

The Roman World

Money by the Pound

ROME. BRONZE AES GRAVE AS. 241–222 B.C.

The first Roman coins are clearly in a class by themselves, and one or more of them certainly deserve to be included in any collection of important coins. They qualify for many reasons; their size alone marks them as being outstanding. The standard aes grave (heavy bronze) coins were about 2-1/2" in diameter and weighed 270 grams (well over one-half pound avoirdupois), and as such, they are some of the largest, thickest, and heaviest of all ancient coins. These Roman coins are also unique in that they were cast rather than being struck, as were nearly all other coins of that period. Speculation is that they were cast in molds made of lava, and their rough surfaces would seem to confirm this conjecture.

Bronze quadrans, plow type. (.79x actual size)

Other special features of these early Roman coins include a multitude of original designs, numerous denominations, and a pattern of downsizing where the diameter was made gradually smaller until even the largest coin was no more than an inch. These pieces are also unusual in that they are made of bronze, and were valued for their metal content. The standard bronze weight was the aes litra, or pound, that was worth about one-fifth of an Attic drachma. Most other coins at that time were made of silver or gold, with only tokens made of bronze.

The earliest Roman bronze money was in the form of lumps or crudely cast bars, called *aes rude* and *aes signatum*. The first recognizable coins were called *aes grave*. They have marks to indicate the denomination in whole or fractional parts of a Roman pound. During much of the third century B.C., most of northern and central Italy made use of cast bronze coins similar to those of Rome. The designs of those coins, and even the weights, were quite different. They seem to have continued in circulation long after the Roman coins developed into more conventional struck pieces made of silver.

The Roman-Oscan pound was based on the Libral standard and was composed of 12 unciae, or ounces. Modern English pound coins, and the very word *pound*, trace their abbreviations (£ and Lb) to the Latin word *libra*, meaning "pound." It is no wonder then that these super-sized coins deserve a place in any list of milestone coins. They are unique in numismatic history.

The earliest Roman aes grave coins displayed images of heads and animals on the obverse, and a spoked wheel on the reverse. The second and slightly more common series shows heads of various Roman deities on the obverse, and the prow of a ship on the reverse.

It is difficult to generalize on the values of these unique coins. Every one is different in some respect and condition is not necessarily as important as overall appearance. They are usually not worn from circulation, but may suffer from being poorly made or badly preserved. The largest pieces are usually the most valuable, and priced around $2,500 and up. Smaller sizes range from $200 to $1,000.

.92x actual size

The Greco-Roman Standard

Rome. Silver Didrachm. 241–235 B.C.

The large lumps of copper or bronze that were used as money in third-century Rome were not acceptable in other regions where more sophisticatedly struck coins were being used. The currencies of southern Italy and Sicily were well-known and desirable trade coins in the region for 300 years prior to the advent of Roman coins. In order to compete the Romans sought to make some of their coins in the image of their neighbors' large and beautiful silver pieces. To do this, they very likely employed itinerant celators who had previously made dies for other cities.

When Roman silver coins first made their appearance, around 280 B.C., they were not only similar in appearance to the well-established Greek-influenced pieces, they were also of similar weight and size. The didrachm and drachm became their standard unit of currency, which lasted until 211 B.C. Those coins were then replaced by a somewhat lighter coin called the *denarius*, which remained the principal coin of the Roman currency system for the following four and a half centuries.

Roman didrachms and drachms of this period play a part in history that sets them apart from other coins of this time, and the standardized Roman monetary system that developed later. They are popular favorites because of their detailed engravings and unique designs. Most prominent is the type with a helmeted head of Mars on the obverse, and a horse's head on the reverse. The most frequently seen type shows the two-faced head of Janus on the obverse, similar to the head used on the large bronze aes grave, and Victory in a galloping quadriga (four-horse chariot) on the reverse. Each of these designs is frequently used on both of the silver denominations that were made prior to the coinage reform in 211.

The artistry on these coins is reminiscent of other silver coins of the period that were made throughout Magna Graecia, and as such, they are collected for their artistic merits as well as being functional parts of the Roman monetary system. Such is not always true of later Roman coins that were apt to be more practical than creative.

Searching for specimens to fill this spot in the history of coinage will be a challenge. The coins are not excessively rare, but finding nice pieces can be difficult. They are seldom seen in dealers' stock, but do occasionally turn up at auction.

Very Fine examples of early drachms and didrachms that were engraved by artisans are often priced at $1,200 to $3,000. The less attractive Janus Head type can often be found with prices under $500. Many of these coins suffer from rough or worn surface conditions, and are worth considerably less.

Roman silver didrachm.
(1.5x actual size)

3x actual size

Choosing a Winner

ROME. SILVER DENARIUS. CIRCA 106 B.C.

No illustrative collection of world coins would be complete without at least one example of the famous Roman silver denarius. With hundreds to choose from, it can be a challenge to select something representative, entertaining, and outstanding. Yet, that is the charm of Roman Republican coins. The various themes used in their designs seem to be almost limitless. Boats, animals, fighting scenes, famous people, and familiar stories are all there for your pick.

Boats, animals, fighting scenes, famous people, and familiar stories are all there for your pick.

The piece shown here is one of my favorites, and one that many collectors find typical of the educational aspects of Republican coins. It was issued sometime around 106 B.C. by P. Licinius Nerva, and is one of the most celebrated types because it depicts the actual voting process in use at that time. The scene shows the political assembly of the Roman people in the comitium (meeting place), where citizens voted on business presented to them by magistrates. The area occupied by the comitium was consecrated ground, like the temple, and was located in front of the senate house in the forum.

The obverse of this denarius shows the helmeted bust of Roma facing left, holding a spear and shield, with the word ROMA on the right. On the reverse is a voting scene showing two citizens casting their ballots in the comitium. One of them is being handed his voting tablet by an attendant who sits behind a screen. The figures are ascending by steps to the bridge, or platform, of the comitium to cast their vote into a basket, having taken their tickets for that purpose from the diribitores, or serutineers, below. The moneyer's name, P NERVA, is shown at the top of the coin.

The comitium was one of two places where assemblies of the people were held in ancient Rome. At a time of voting, citizens were given electoral tickets for either making some law, or for the election of a consul, or some other public function. There are existing descriptions of the voting procedure, but few contemporary illustrations of the scene other than those on coins.

Pictorial denarii of the Roman Republic are not scarce, but some of the scenes are more desirable than others. Of all choices, the famous voting scene is one of the most popular and as such is slightly more costly than those with less interesting designs. Finding a suitable specimen will be a challenge. Some are poorly struck, worn, or off-center, and they are something that a dealer will not have in stock all the time. Patience is key to locating a nice denarius with this design. When located, a Very Fine example should be available for something less than $200.

3.53x actual size

Goddess of Money

ROME. SILVER DENARIUS OF T. CARISIUS. CIRCA 45 B.C.

Roman Republican pictorial denarii of the second and first centuries B.C. hold special interest for collectors because they depict so many different contemporary scenes. Many of the things that are shown on these coins are not seen in any other art form. They inform us about legends, deities, people, and events that might otherwise be lost to history.

It is important to include one or more of these interesting coins in any selection of historical milestone events as an illustration of the kind of money used by the Romans for nearly two centuries. They are also delightful examples of the innovative designs used to show how people of that time respected their heritage and tried to preserve imagery for future generations to learn from and admire. These coins served a function similar to books and pictures: to circulate messages to the general public.

Each collector will probably find a personal favorite among the many designs in this long series of coins. One stands out so prominently that nearly everyone enjoys collecting a specimen to illustrate a very special element of numismatic history. The design on the coin shown here tells the story of the origin of the word *money*, and shows implements used in the making of coins at that time. The unique design was the inspiration of the moneyer T. Carisius, who ordered the coin to be struck somewhere around 45 B.C.

On the obverse of this silver denarius is a representation of the goddess Juno Moneta with the legend MONETA to the left of her head. The reverse depicts coining implements that include an anvil with a punch-die above, between tongs and hammer. T. CARISIVS, the moneyer's name, is above. This design memorializes the Roman mint that was adjacent to the temple dedicated to Juno Moneta on the Arx summit of the Capitoline Hill.

The mint was under the patronage of the goddess Juno Moneta (the Advisor), and her name eventually became the origin of the word *money*. Students of ancient coinage methods find it interesting to see the types of tools that were used in the production of coins at that time. Some scholars see the central design as an anvil with the cap of Vulcan (god of fire and the forge) above, but it is more likely intended to represent a conical die. A hand-striking method would have been used to impress a coin. The obverse die was imbedded in an anvil, and the reverse was held above, perhaps with the tongs shown at the left. A hammer, shown on the right, was used to strike the blank of metal that was placed between the two dies.

These coins served a function similar to books and pictures: to circulate messages to the general public.

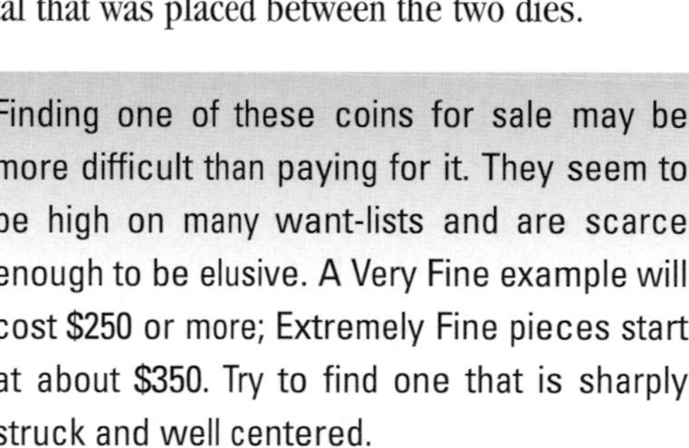

Finding one of these coins for sale may be more difficult than paying for it. They seem to be high on many want-lists and are scarce enough to be elusive. A Very Fine example will cost $250 or more; Extremely Fine pieces start at about $350. Try to find one that is sharply struck and well centered.

3.33x actual size

Beware the Ides of March

ROME. SILVER DENARIUS OF BRUTUS. 42 B.C.

If any single coin deserves to be called the most important and significant of all remarkable issues, it has to be the silver denarius made by Marcus Junius Brutus in the summer of 42 B.C. The design on this coin specifically alludes to the assassination of Julius Caesar, by Brutus himself, and shows a liberty cap flanked by daggers. The inscription EID MAR is an abbreviation for *Eidibus Martiis*, which refers to the Ides of March, the date when Caesar was assassinated.

Brutus denarius with the head of Libertas, 54 B.C. (1.5x actual size)

Many advanced collectors revere this coin as a significant goal for desirability and esteem. Unfortunately, the few treasured surviving specimens are either in museums, or may be priced well above ordinary financial resources. It is a major numismatic event when one appears on the market, and when that does happen, the auction bidding is sure to be intense.

Brutus was the son of Caesar's former mistress, Servilia. He began his political career in 58 B.C., and as triumvir monetalis he issued coins shortly thereafter, demonstrating his strong republican views. Those coins, which show Libertas and portraits of his ancestors (who overthrew the last Etruscan king of Rome), make good collector substitutes for the nearly unobtainable Eid Mar rarities.

In 49 B.C. Brutus joined with Pompey in a civil war against Caesar. Surprisingly, after their defeat, Brutus was granted a pardon and appointed governor of Gaul in 46 B.C. He later joined in the conspiracy against Caesar, and with Cassius became one of the principals in the well-known assassination of Caesar on March 15, 44 B.C. Faced with general disgrace, he was declared a "public enemy" by the Senate and was forced to leave Rome the following month. Although many senators plotted against Caesar, they are represented by only two daggers on this commemorative coin, and the portrait of Brutus alone emphasizes his role as the primary conspirator.

Brutus's transgressions were soon (mostly) forgiven and by the next year he was appointed governor of Crete, but after establishment of the triumvirate, he again joined forces with Cassius. In the summer of 42 B.C. they marched through Macedonia and won their first battle against Octavian. The elated Brutus sought to propagandize the event and inflate his own image by issuing the famous coins boasting of his assassination of Caesar. In an ironic twist of fate, as his power waned, Brutus committed suicide in October of that year—using the very same dagger that had killed the noblest Roman of all.

The coins of Brutus show what are considered to be his most realistic representations. It is no wonder that the famous Eid Mar denarii stand out so prominently among all coins of the ages for their desirability

3.53x actual size

and importance, and why they are so eagerly sought by collectors.

Recent sales of Eid Mar coins of Brutus have brought prices in the $30,000 to $60,000 range, depending on condition. Worn specimens are occasionally offered for sale, but even the poorest will achieve a substantial price. Substitute pieces will make a more affordable choice for most collectors. A denarius of L. Servius Rufus issued in 41 B.C. shows the lifelike head of Brutus on the obverse, and the Dioscuri (the legendary Castor and Pollux, sons of Jupiter) standing, holding spear and sword, on the reverse. These are sometimes available for $1,000 or more. A second choice that is usually more readily available is a coin issued by Brutus in 54 B.C. with the head of Libertas on the obverse, and his illustrious ancestors walking in procession with lectors on the reverse. This type refers to the prominence of his lineage and his own patriotic devotion to the freedom of the Republic. Coins of this interesting type are generally valued from $200 to $300. Another coin issued by Brutus around the same time shows the bare head of his ancestor L. Junius Brutus, who was consul in 509 B.C., on the obverse, and the bearded head of Servilius Ahala on the reverse. A Very Fine specimen of this type will likely be priced at $250 to $350.

Sextus Pompey, who issued this silver denarius, was the son of Pompey the Great. He tried and nearly gained control of Rome following Caesar's assassination, but was overthrown by Octavian, who became the first emperor of Rome.

Brutus issued commemorative coins in conjunction with his office as monetales. This silver denarius struck circa 58 B.C. honors two of his illustrious ancestors.

It is a major numismatic event when one appears on the market, and the auction bidding is sure to be intense.

Noblest Roman of All

Rome. Silver Denarius of Julius Caesar. 44 B.C.

It is difficult to imagine anyone who is not familiar with the exploits of Julius Caesar. He was the undisputed master of Rome, and displayed an amazing breadth of interests and talents. He reformed civic administration in Rome and throughout Italy with urban renewal, colonization, and the extension of Roman citizenship into the provinces. His most lasting accomplishments were the founding of the first public library and the refinement of the Roman calendar, which is still in use today with only minor modifications.

Amazingly, Julius Caesar is not best known as the brilliant strategist, military leader, and reformer that he was. His more familiar legacy has been memorialized in the play *Julius Caesar* by William Shakespeare, in his dalliance with Cleopatra, and in his tragic death by assassination on the Ides of March in 44 B.C. Regardless of how he is remembered, he remains larger than life as a heroic leader and historic character whose coins are treasured by all who include them in their collections.

Elephant-type denarius of Julius Caesar. (1.5x actual size)

Although not without his critics, Julius Caesar certainly deserves to have one or more of his coins singled out as representative of this important chapter in history. Many different types of coins were issued during his brief stint as dictator from 49 to 44 B.C. None of these coins are very common, but a few are regularly available despite heavy demand.

Caesar was born in 100 B.C. to an important Roman family. He began his political career by opposing Marius and Sulla, each of whom had led armies against Rome. Caesar's first major success was his election, in 63 B.C., to the office of Pontifex Maximus, or high priest of the Roman religion. Two years later he formed the First Triumvirate, a private political alliance with Crassus and Pompey. Asserting his new power, he assumed governorship of Gaul, which comprised northern Italy and southern France. He then extended Roman control into Germany and Britain.

Pompey's growing power in Rome caused a rift that forced Caesar to return to reestablish his control there. In 49 B.C. he crossed the Rubicon with his legions and captured the city. The civil war between Caesar and the Pompeians lasted for four years, with Caesar pursuing Pompey to Egypt where he spent the summer with the young queen Cleopatra. By March of 45 B.C. Caesar had made himself undisputed master of the Roman world and began his extensive reforms, which won him the admiration of many Roman citizens. His downfall came a year later when in February of 44 B.C. he was appointed perpetual dictator of Rome. One of his first acts was to commission coins to be minted with his portrait, an act that was without precedent. This open show of unlimited power provoked the conspiracy against him that culminated in his assassination a month later (on the Ides of March) by Brutus, Cassius, and others.

3.33x actual size

Many different types of coins were issued under Caesar's authority. Those made with his portrait stand out from all others and are clearly the favorites among collectors. They are scarce and difficult to acquire because they were made for such a short period of time and because of the constant demand for portrait pieces of the first 12 caesars. A Fine-condition denarius will show a recognizable portrait and may be purchased for about $600. Very Fine or better pieces generally sell for upwards of $1,000, and for an Extremely Fine coin, expect to compete with museums and advanced collectors willing to expend several thousand dollars. The most common coins of Julius Caesar are the so-called elephant denarii made by a mobile military unit traveling with Caesar during his campaign against Pompey the Great between 49 and 48 B.C. These show an elephant trampling a serpent above the word CAESAR on the obverse. The reverse shows ritual implements of the Pontifex Maximus, his lifelong office. A Very Fine example of this interesting coinage will cost somewhere around $400, or a bit less if one settles for the usual off-center or carelessly struck pieces. Other interesting coins of Caesar include those struck by his traveling military mints in his campaigns against the Pompeians in 48 B.C., and in Africa from 47 to 46 B.C. Both of these are occasionally available at prices around $500 for Extremely Fine specimens.

On this denarius of Julius Caesar the Roman numerals LII, left of Clementia's head, indicate his age (52) at the time the coins were made in 48 B.C., two years before his death.

Roman silver portrait denarius of Octavian and Marc Antony, commemorating the establishment of the Second Triumvirate in November of 43 B.C.

One of Caesar's first acts—commissioning coins with his own portrait—was an act without precedent.

Nero the Fiddler

Rome. Copper As of Nero. A.D. 64

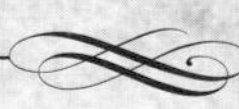

The "bad guys" seem to have made their mark in history just as prominently as saints and reformers. In any list of the worst, the Roman emperor Nero would be found close to, if not at, the top. He was definitely not the sort of person you would enjoy knowing as a personal acquaintance. He was, however, the kind of a character who can best be remembered through his coinage, and he belongs in any numismatic hall of fame. His life is a story to be pondered rather than honored.

Denarius of Nero.
(1.5x actual size)

Nero became emperor of Rome in A.D. 54 at the tender age of 17. He inherited the title upon the death of his mother's uncle, Emperor Claudius, who was probably poisoned by her. He began to show his erratic and unpredictable behavior soon after gaining authority to control the empire, and built a magnificent palace known as the Golden House. From that point on, his excesses became legendary to the point were he was dreaded by everyone in the Roman world. His intolerance of religious autonomy was the cause of Christian persecution, and the Jewish Revolt of A.D. 66. Unrest in the provinces soon led to uprisings in Spain and Gaul, and ultimately to Nero's suicide and the election of Galba as emperor in A.D. 68.

Despite the difficulties of his administration, Nero had a decisive effect on the artistic character of the empire. He had an abiding interest in the arts, and fancied himself to be a skillful actor, musician, and poet. His coins reflect a quality of engraving seen in few others before or since, and realistically depict the emperor at various ages. His pudgy features and artificial hairstyle are unmistakable marks of his later issues, which give these coins great character.

Nero's reign is also noteworthy for changes he made to the Roman monetary system. From A.D. 54 to 64, he maintained the old standards of weight and fineness for gold and silver coins. In 64, the weight was significantly reduced, and a new series of bronze coins was introduced. Throughout his reign many different denominations and designs were used to proclaim his interests and accomplishments. Collectors find them enjoyable for their bold representations and artistry, and consequently, they are always in high demand.

The copper coin shown here illustrates Nero's temperament for the arts, showing him dressed in the robes of Apollo and playing the lyre. That was one of his special "talents" and he frequently forced audiences to listen to him perform for hours. It is possible that the scene on this coin could have sparked the legend that Nero fiddled while Rome burned, but there is no basis in fact for thinking he really did that. A fire did burn much of the city in A.D. 64, and some believe that it may have been purposely started to rid the city of unwanted slums. The fire also served to incriminate Christians, who were accused of starting the conflagration.

Coins of Nero are too numerous and varied to make precise comments about average values. Attractive copper and bronze pieces usually cost from $100 to $500. Well-struck silver denarii start at about $500 to $800.

2.11x actual size

Will the Real Emperor Please Stand?

Rome. Silver Denarius of Galba. A.D. 68–69

Nero's excesses earned him the enmity of both the Senate and the army, and in A.D. 68 he was compelled to commit suicide. The loss left the empire without direction and set the stage for a civil war to determine who would rule. Four different Roman generals managed to assume the title of emperor over the course of the following year. This unusual period is called the "Year of the Four Emperors," and deserves to be represented with a numismatic reminder of the events. The four Roman emperors were Galba, Otho, Vitellius, and Vespasian. Senator Julius Vindex was a relatively minor fifth participant who supported Galba, but he was killed in May of A.D. 68. Each emperor issued coins in one form or another to declare a claim to the throne.

The civil war that lasted from June of 68 to December of 69 was the first since Marc Antony's death in 30 B.C. It was one of many civic disturbances that had plagued Rome since the Marsic Confederation uprising of 90 to 88 B.C. This one had a successful ending when the Senate acknowledged Vespasian as emperor on the 21st of December 69, the very same year that had begun with Galba on the throne. Vespasian's rule was long and stable, and he died of natural causes as emperor in A.D. 79, with the famous last words, "Dear me, I must be turning into a god."

During the civil war period, several coins were issued with propaganda messages from the hopeful contenders for the throne. All of them are considered to be scarce or rare, and all are relatively costly. The same is true for the officially issued coins of the various emperors who ruled for only a few months before being deposed. Gold, silver, and copper coins were issued by all four emperors, and are always eagerly sought by collectors. They are particularly important to those who try to assemble sets of coins of the 12 caesars made famous by the literary work of Suetonius. In that indispensable work, one can find the stories of all the early Roman emperors who ruled from 50 B.C. to A.D. 96. It is highly recommended reading for additional information about the personal lives of these important figures and their role in history.

Silver denarii of Otho (top) and Vitellius (bottom). (1.5x actual size)

Civil war issues are not often found in superior condition and may command prices starting at $1,000. Inferior pieces are more often available, and may be priced at about $500 and up. Coins of Galba, Otho, and Vitellius are often available for prices from $500 to $1,200. Those of Vespasian are much more common and will cost around $300 for specimens in Very Fine to Extremely Fine condition.

3.53x actual size

Sold to the Highest Bidder

ROME. FOURRÉ SILVER DENARIUS. DIDIUS JULIANUS. A.D. 193

Mutinous soldiers put the throne up for auction, selling imperial authority to the highest bidder.

The name Didius Julianus will not be familiar to very many who are not collectors of ancient Roman coins. Yet, he is one of those colorful characters whose career was bizarre enough to earn him a unique place in numismatic history. He is one of several emperors who ruled for only a few months and issued only a limited number of coins. All of Julianus's issues are scarce and in constant demand by those who try to collect at least one coin of each emperor. They are also distinct reminders of his obsession for power, and the result of a scheme gone awry.

Didius Severus Julianus was born in A.D. 133 to a prominent family in Milan. He was privileged to have a distinguished public career, and held consulship during the troubled years of the civil-war strife in Rome under the brief reign of Emperor Pertinax. Civic duties undoubtedly brought him into contact with disgruntled soldiers who were plotting an assassination of the emperor. The thought must have stirred his ambition to assume the throne himself.

The Praetorian Guard carried out their mutinous plot on March 28, 193, by murdering Pertinax in his palace. They then conspired to put the imperial throne up for auction, and to sell the power to the highest bidder. It was not unheard of at that time for a new emperor to offer payment to soldiers in an effort to secure their loyalty, but actively seeking the highest bidder was a bolder and greedier maneuver than usual.

Didius was encouraged to bid on rights to the throne by his wife, Manlia Scantilla, and their daughter Didia Clara. It is said that he was also encouraged by Flavius Sulpicianus, father of the widowed wife of Pertinax. Spurred on by their enthusiasm, Didius placed the winning bid of 25,000 bronze sestertii for each soldier. It was an enormous sum that was never paid in full, but it did secure for him the power of the throne.

The appalling acts of all those involved aroused resentment throughout the provinces, and a call for revenge was issued. Governors in three separate regions answered the plea for justice. In Britain, Clodius Albinus was proclaimed emperor, while in Pannonia, Septimius Severus was selected to rule, and in Syria, Pescennius Niger was acknowledged by his troops. Clodius Severus was the first to arrive in Rome in his march on the capital where he was warmly welcomed.

Julianus tried to negotiate a compromise with Severus, but was unsuccessful and quickly deposed by the Senate. Facing reprisals on all fronts, Julianus hid in his palace but was found and murdered by a soldier barely two months after his ascension to the throne. Stripped of title and wealth, his wife and their daughter died in relative obscurity.

All coins of Didius Julianus are scarce and costly. Silver denarii are sometimes available in Fine at $1,500 or more. The specimen shown here was made of silver-coated copper to cheat the public.

3.17x actual size

A Millennium Celebration

Rome. Silver Antoninianus. Philip I. A.D. 244–249

In an empire whose coinage lasted for hundreds of years, it is difficult to select one emperor or event that stands out significantly above the others. This is especially true of the later emperors, many of whom led peaceful lives or even died of natural causes. Still, at least one coin should be singled out to highlight the era of third-century Rome. One standout event that comes easily to mind is the celebration of the millennium of the founding of the city of Rome. The big event happened during the reign of Philip I, in A.D. 248.

Legend says that the Eternal City was founded in 753 B.C. by Romulus and his twin brother Remus. They were sons of Mars, and as young boys were abandoned on the Palatine Hill where they were suckled by a she-wolf. Romulus is supposed to have built the city and named it after himself, although some versions of the story claim that Remus originally had attempted to have the city bear his name. The she-wolf has remained a symbol of Rome ever since, and her image is frequently seen in art, alone or with the twins.

This fanciful tale does not reflect the more historically accurate account of the area originally being inhabited by various tribes early in the eighth century B.C., and their domination by the Etruscans who built the settlement that would one day become Rome. The city is built on the famous Seven Hills, and has been one of the most important cities in the world for more than 2,750 years.

Roman citizens were aware that the millennium anniversary of the founding of the city would occur in the year 248. They were proud of the longevity and delighted when Emperor Philip I announced there would be *saeculares*, or secular games, to celebrate the thousandth year since the founding of Rome. The event was widely publicized through his coins that bore inscriptions and references to the celebration. Some of these have the inscription SAECVLARES AVGG, along with the figure of Roma or the she-wolf, while others show animals that were exhibited in the amphitheater as part of the festivities.

One or more of these commemorative coins should be part of any representative collection of important Roman pieces. They are all relatively common and readily available thanks to hoards of coins from this period that have been found in Italy, England, and elsewhere. Both bronze and silver coins of this emperor are easily obtainable. The debased silver coin of this period, the antoninianus, was equal to two denarii.

Philip was married to Otacilia Severa, a Christian who persuaded Philip to accompany her on visits to the bishop of Antioch. They bore a daughter and a son, Philip II, who was given the title of *Augustus* as a child. Both Philip and his son were slain by his own soldiers in 249 during a revolt that favored Trajanus Decius, the man who had been proclaimed emperor by the army in Pannonia.

The 1,000-year anniversary of Rome was widely publicized through Philip's coins, which referred to the millennium celebrations.

Antoninianii of Philip are usually available in Very Fine or better condition for $25 to $30. Commemorative designs are sometimes priced a bit higher.

2.43x actual size

CHAPTER 4

Money in Medieval Europe

Byzantine Bronzes

Byzantine Empire. Justinian I. Bronze 40 Nummia. 527–565

Coins of the Byzantine Empire began with sweeping reform that distinguished them from the dilapidated Roman coins of the late fifth century, which no longer served the needs of everyday citizens. The main feature of the reform, enacted in 498, was the introduction of new bronze coins that were clearly marked with values showing the number of nummia in each denomination. Gold and silver coins retained the same Roman denominations, but the designs were somewhat changed.

Intrigues of court, debauchery, greed, and cruelty permeated the Byzantine Empire and influenced its coinage.

Byzantine coins are so distinctive that they appeal to many collectors as something apart from any other coinage that may have come before or after. Their role in monetary history cannot be ignored and must be represented by at least a few carefully chosen pieces. The operative phrase here is "carefully chosen." Byzantine coins are not great works of art. The condition of these pieces is often wretched, and they are apt to be difficult to attribute and understand. Couple that with the extent of the series that lasted for nearly 1,000 years, from about 491 to 1450, and you have a rather ungainly challenge.

Even the exact time span of the empire is open to dispute, so collectors must make some personal choices about what is appropriate and representative for this period. The one thing certain about these unusual coins is that they are fascinating. A good starting point for adding at least one specimen to your collection would be a bronze coin of Emperor Justinian I, who ruled from 527 to 565. He was a learned man of relatively good character, albeit sometimes unjustly reputed to be vain, heartless, and mean. His coins are numerous, commonly available, and relatively inexpensive. Moreover, the design and execution of these pieces are generally superior to most of the later issues.

Byzantine coins have much to offer collectors in the way of numismatic side-trips. They were made in many denominations and sizes, sometimes with odd shapes. Satellite mints made pieces that are identified by mintmarks, and some issues are dated. Nearly all have indications of their Christian derivation. Some are interesting for the monarchs who made them, with appellations such as Leo the Wise, Michael the Drunkard, Justinian II the Slit-Nosed, and many others. Intrigues of court, debauchery, greed, and unbridled cruelty permeated the Byzantine Empire and influenced its coinage. Any numismatic investigation of these coins will be a rewarding journey.

The coin of Justinian I shown here is one of the largest of all Byzantine issues. It is also one of the most attractive bronze coins. Gold pieces are far superior in execution and style, and are surprisingly inexpensive. Silver coins are generally scarcer than either gold or bronze. Some diligent searching will turn up a representative piece that will be both attractive and exciting to commemorate this point in history.

1.5x actual size

Those who collect Byzantine coins have a wide range of types, styles, and themes from which to choose. One popular course is to assemble representative coins from as many emperors as possible. A less ambitious choice is to find coins of different denominations or mints. Highly motivated collectors might save not only all the above, but also coins of every date and mint.

The challenge of collecting from the Byzantine Empire is deepened by the thousand-year history of its coinage, and the unusual blend of Roman, Greek, and religious customs that permeate its frequently changing designs and styles. This, coupled with the wear and tear imposed on the coins through prolonged circulation, has left many pieces that seem hardly fit to accompany other ancient examples of numismatic artistry. Yet, Byzantine coins are what they are, and they have an attraction all their own that makes the occasional choice specimen all the more rare and appealing.

Shown here is a typical example of the rugged fabric and artistry of the first of the Byzantine bronze coins, minted during the reign of Anastasius I, who ruled from 491 to 518. The Constantinople "mint-mark" CON is in the exergue, below the letter M (signifying the denomination, 40 nummi or one follis). No fewer than 27 different mints made coins during the time of the Byzantine Empire. Other coins representative of this series are shown for comparison; numerous denominations in gold, silver, and copper were used throughout the series.

> Byzantine bronze coins are common and inexpensive, but apt to be worn, misshapen, and ugly. Patience is needed to locate a piece worthy of the $30 to $70 that it will cost. Expect to pay $200 or more for anything attractive or in high grade.

Copper follis (M=40) of Anastasius I. (Actual size)

Reduced-size copper follis of Leo VI, the Wise (886–912). (Actual size)

Typical copper follis of Heraclius (613–638), overstruck on an older cut-down coin. (Actual size)

Silver coins, such as this miliaresion of Leo III (717–741), often show a cross or other religious symbol, and a lengthy inscription for identification. (Actual size)

A gold solidus of Justin II (565–578) exemplifies the care that was taken to produce a much finer quality precious-metal coinage. (Actual size)

Byzantine Gold

Byzantine Empire. Justinian II. Gold Solidus. 692–695

The most attractive Byzantine coins are their lovely gold pieces. The standard denomination was the solidus, which had been carried over from the Roman coin of the same name. A majority of the gold coins made prior to 700 have a bust of the emperor on the obverse and a cross or angel on the reverse. Most of these pieces were struck at the mint in Constantinople. With the end of iconoclastic restrictions, a bust of Christ was often shown on the obverse, sometimes with that of the emperor on the reverse. During the reign of Constantine IX, in 1042, a new-style gold piece called the *hyperpyron* was introduced. These coins have the unusual feature of being larger in diameter and cup-shaped.

Justinian II distinguished his coins by adding to them a portrait of Jesus of Nazareth.

Fortunately for collectors, many Byzantine gold coins have survived the ages and are some of the more inexpensive of all antique gold coins. This is equally true of the solidus and the semissis (half solidus), and the tremissis (third solidus), as well as many of the later cup-shaped coins that are commonly called *scyphate*. They enjoy the enviable position of being interesting, unusual, attractive, and affordable.

Among the most popular and desirable Byzantine gold coins are those of Justinian II, whose first rule lasted from A.D. 685 to 695. He distinguished his coins by adding to them a portrait of Jesus of Nazareth. Just why the emperor did this is still somewhat of a mystery, but it gave the world the first numismatic image of Christ, and popularized a representation that has become a standard icon ever since. The romantic image was taken from earlier Byzantine art, and is based on a reasonable concept of what Jesus may have looked like. No contemporary image of Christ is known to exist, so we are left to wonder how accurate this, or any, rendering may be.

The Trullan Synod of 692 had decreed that in the future Christ should be portrayed in human rather than symbolic form. Perhaps the use of this new portrait was a result of Justinian's attempt to promulgate such an image. Whatever his motives, the portrait helped fan the raging controversy between those who favored the use of such imagery, and the iconoclasts who sought to dispense with all such religious representations.

The portrait shown on these coins is that of a gentle man with a short beard and long hair. The image is poignant and has a regal quality. Behind his head can be seen a cross. In his hand is a book of the Gospels. On the reverse of this piece, the emperor is shown standing and holding a cross potent (formed by capital Ts joined at their bases) on three steps.

As commendable as this design may be, it is no indication of the character of Justinian II. Known for being cruel and despicable, Justinian seems to have been despised by everyone in the empire, and with good reason. He was also unbalanced and immature, and had a quick temper. Most onerous of all was his

3x actual size

obsession with extracting taxes to fund the spiraling cost of managing his empire. It is said that his collectors hung delinquent taxpayers head down over fires, and even had the emperor's mother flogged, without protest from the emperor. His 10-year reign of terror was overthrown in 695 by a revolt. To ensure the end of his supremacy, the insurgents slit his nose, thus rendering him imperfect and therefore unfit for the throne. This act of mutilation may have been merciful, but the new emperor Leontius came to regret this decision soon enough—he assumed the purple for only the next three years. Unrest at home and abroad continued to plague the empire, and the continuing revolt in 698 resulted in Tiberius being given the throne. Leontius then had his own nose slit, and was confined to a monastery.

While these colorful events would seem to signal the end of this eventful chapter in Byzantine history, it was only the beginning. Justinian continued to plot his revenge for the next several years, and rose again to power in 705 with an even more sadistic reign of terror. His second reign also produced another numismatic treasure—a new portrait of Christ, which is discussed in the following narrative.

The revised portrait of Christ is quite different from the first design, and shows an image that looks more like the emperor himself. It is, however, that of a young man more about the age of 30, and near the end of his life. It may in fact be more realistic than the first design, which seems to show a much older man. These two unusual coins stand out among all other Byzantine designs because they contain the first and only portraits of Christ that were used until the end of the iconoclastic movement in the middle of the ninth century. When the practice was once again introduced, similar designs were used on many Byzantine coins in gold, silver, and copper, and always in a manner similar to the first portrait style.

The gold solidus of Justinian II with a facing head of Christ is an extremely popular coin type. High-grade specimens are not uncommon, but finding one that is well struck, centered, and with a pleasing portrait is difficult. Many are struck on undersized planchets and missing part of the design, or are made from worn dies. Very few show signs of excessive wear, perhaps because they have been saved since ancient times as religious icons. Prices range from about $1,250 for the less attractive pieces to $5,000 for a real gem. For maximum satisfaction, try to locate one in your price range that is as representative as possible.

Copper follis of John I (969–976), showing a traditional bust of Christ. (1.5x actual size)

Copper follis of Theodora (1055–1056), with a half-length figure of Christ. (Actual size)

Justinian Returns

Byzantine Empire. Justinian II. Gold Solidus. 705–711

The expression "a bad penny always returns" could well have originated with Justinian II. Ten years after being deposed, Justinian conspired to regain the throne. It is believed that to accomplish this, he wore a golden cover over his slit nose to hide his deformity. His second turn as ruler in 705 was much to the regret of all concerned. His first act was to include his young son Tiberius in his court. Some of his new coins display their joint busts. In retribution for his earlier dethronement, everyone suspected of playing a part was put to death, tortured, or blinded. A new reign of terror began with more intensity than the old, and lasted for the next six years.

The design of this coin is as intriguing today as it must have been 1,300 years ago.

Once again, faced with the emperor's insane behavior, the army revolted, and elected an Armenian named Philippicus as their new ruler. At that point, en masse, everyone deserted Justinian, who was then seized and beheaded. This, however, is not the lasting way that numismatists remember this remarkable chapter in Byzantine history. Despite his evil doings, Justinian favored the world with another innovative bust of Christ on his coins.

The revised portrait of Christ that is shown on the gold solidus minted during the second reign of Justinian II is significantly different from that used on the coins of his first reign. The earlier portrait, discussed in the previous narrative, was traditional and in keeping with familiar Byzantine iconography in showing the features of Christ Pantokrator (the Ruler of All). The second design shows a much younger head of Jesus.

Inspiration for the revised portrait is believed by some to have come from a drawing that was supposedly made during the lifetime of Christ, but there is little evidence to support that theory. The facing bust on the revised coins shows a youthful countenance with a stubbly beard and short curly hair. Jesus' right hand is raised in blessing, and the Gospel is held in his left hand. A cross is behind his head, all of which is surrounded by the legend. On the reverse is a crowned bust of Justinian, either alone or with his son Tiberius. On the former piece, he is holding the cross potent in one hand, and the patriarchal globus, inscribed PAX, in the other.

The design of this coin is as intriguing today as it must have been 1,300 years ago. It had to be a tour-de-force of propaganda to introduce confidence in the despised emperor, and proclaim his support of Christianity and peace. Yet it was all to no avail. He was soon overthrown by Philippicus, who favored the iconoclastic ideology. After that time, the portrait of Christ was excluded from all coinage, and was not seen again until the reign of Michael III from 842 to 867, when the iconoclastic movement had ended.

Coins of Justinian II with the curly-headed bust of Christ may be a bit scarcer than those with the traditional bust, but are not quite as popular with most collectors. Prices are slightly lower, with well-struck Extremely Fine specimens selling at about $2,000.

3x actual size

Trouble in the Empire

Seljuk Turks. Kay-Khusrau I. Bronze Folus. 1192–1199
Sicily. Roger I. Bronze Trifollaro. 1072–1101

The Byzantine period covered the time span from about A.D. 450 to 1450, and corresponded almost exactly to what is called the Middle Ages, depending on which chronology one chooses. During that time a huge amount of energy was spent fighting wars that only served to make everyone miserable, hostile, and without any clear vision of the past or future. The so-called Holy Crusades pitted one religion against another, and worked to the detriment of both. It was a time of unrest and despair, marked with little artistic achievement.

As a consequence of those struggles, the quality of coins suffered along with everything else. The tenor of the times is reflected in the poor imagery of numismatic art, and many collectors ignore the entire era as unworthy of consideration. That attitude is unfortunate because the coins of this period not only have a unique character, but are also historically important and often associated with famous people who merit being remembered through surviving numismatic artifacts.

The coins that are shown here to represent this period are not necessarily *typical* medieval pieces. They are, however, some of the most popular designs because they show action between opposing warriors of the Crusades. Or at least they are idealistic images of those who fought for their beliefs. Like many coins of those troubled times, they are carelessly made and rarely found in choice condition. A coin of Romanus IV, the Byzantine emperor, would nicely represent the time of the beginning of the Crusades, but would lack the sensation and popularity of the pieces here illustrated.

One of the major reasons for launching the Crusades was the rise in power of the Seljuk Turks. This was of concern to the rulers of the Byzantine Empire not only because it threatened their independence, but because it also compromised the safety of the pilgrims who were frequent visitors to their holy sites. In 1070 Jerusalem was overrun by the Seljuks, and in the next year, Emperor Romanus IV was defeated and taken captive by the Turks. By 1092 many of the metropolitan Byzantine cities in Asia were overrun, and the emperor requested assistance from the pope to repel the invaders and rescue the Holy Sepulcher. War soon broke out between the Byzantine Empire and the Normans of Sicily, and by 1095, the full Crusades were underway.

The coins illustrated here, while not typical, are popular favorites of this time period. The Seljuk bronze folus of Kay-Khusrau will cost only about $125, but may be difficult to locate. His silver coins (without the action scene) are sometimes more readily available for about $200. Very Fine condition is the average for most of these pieces. The same is true for the trifollaro of Roger I of Sicily. Do not hold out for superb condition; be happy to find one in Very Fine condition for $350.

These popular coins show action between opposing warriors at the time of the Crusades.

1.96x and 1.67x actual size

Off to War

Crusaders. Grand Masters of the Order of St. John at Rhodes. Jean Fernandez de Heredia. Silver Gigliato. 1372–1396

At the end of the 10th century, the spread of Islam had abated and a comparatively stable state of affairs existed between Muslims, Jews, and Christians. Pilgrimages were allowed to the holy sites in Jerusalem, which at that time were under Muslim rule. This stable situation began to change with the aggressive expansion of the Turks, who were attacking Christian pilgrims on their way to the Holy Land. The uncertainties of travel were of great concern to all European Christians, for whom pilgrimages were an important part of their religion. With the Byzantine Empire in peril from the Seljuk Turks, Emperor Alexius sent a request to Pope Urban II in Rome for help.

The grand masters issued a series of attractive coins, among the most popular of all Crusader pieces.

Concern for the safety of Christian pilgrims led to the founding of a religious society known as the Order of St. John of Jerusalem. The original function of the order was to operate a hospice for pilgrims traveling to the Holy Land, and to assist with safeguarding their passage and welfare. In 1009 the Fatimid caliph al-Hakim bi-Amr Allah sacked the pilgrimage hospice in Jerusalem and destroyed the Church of the Holy Sepulcher. It was an event that prompted approval from the pope to retaliate against the Muslims, and sparked the Crusades. Over time, the Order of St. John became more militant and took an active part in the combative campaigns.

Hostilities worsened over the following 50 years, and by 1063 Pope Alexander II had given papal blessing to Iberian Christians in their wars against the Muslims, and granted indulgences to those Christians killed in battle. The stage was thus set for the Byzantine emperor's new appeal for help, which was readily granted. In 1095, war was declared against the Turks and the crusaders marched to Jerusalem.

The Christians eventually lost the Holy City in 1197, and the Order of St. John moved to Acre in Palestine. In 1310, when the Crusades ended in defeat, the order moved again, this time to the island of Rhodes, where it remained a military power in the region until 1523. During this time the grand masters, who headed the order, issued a series of colorful coins that are among the most attractive of all Crusader pieces. They share a common design on the reverse, and on the obverse is an image of each successive grand master kneeling before a cross. On his shoulder is the cross patch given by the pope and in the right field is his identifying coat of arms.

Silver gigliati of the grand masters are popular for their large size, fine workmanship, and interesting designs. They were issued from 1319 to 1421 through successive grand masters of the Order of the Hospital of Saint John of Jerusalem at Rhodes. Typical specimens are usually in Very Fine or slightly better condition; few are any better, and many are weakly struck, although usually not badly worn. An attractive specimen will cost about $400.

2.07x actual size

Cheers for Saint Louis

France. Louis IX. Silver Gros Tournois. 1226–1270

The disastrous Crusades lasted for 200 years, and comprised eight significant campaigns. The seventh, organized and led by King Louis IX of France, lasted from 1249 to 1252. The eighth and final assault by the Christians, in 1270, was also under the leadership of King Louis. Both of these efforts ended in defeat with Louis spending much of his time living at the court of the Crusader kingdom in Acre. During the eighth crusade he went to the aid of the remnants of the Crusader states in Syria and Tunis, where he spent only two months before dying.

In 1291, when Acre fell, Christian rule in the Holy Land virtually ended. During the various battles of the Crusades, there were many atrocities by both Christians and Muslims. In the end Muslims won more battles and eventually the war, taking control of Palestine and Jerusalem for the next several hundred years.

The fame of this French king came not from his exploits in the Crusades, but rather because of the way he ruled his kingdom and conducted his life. Louis IX was especially kind to the poor, and beloved by his subjects. He was considered the very model of an ideal Christian monarch, and gained the respect of all of his European contemporaries. His participation in the wars was precipitated by his devotion to religious duty and not necessarily reflective of his military competence. His reputation of righteousness and fairness was well known while he was alive, and he was an able arbiter in quarrels among the rulers of Europe. His outstanding pious character was such that he was canonized by Pope Boniface VIII and proclaimed a saint in 1297.

As an able ruler, Louis initiated many reforms and benefits for the betterment of his subjects. A very noticeable change was made in the nation's coinage when he introduced a new denomination known as the gros tournois. This coin was much larger than the usual silver pieces of that time, and was a very welcome bolster to the growing economy. It became such a convenient and popular denomination that its weight, size, and fineness were frequently imitated throughout Europe, and became a standard for many years.

At a time when many European silver coins were small, badly made, and of questionable fineness, the French gros tournois was a well-liked and useful innovation. As the first of their kind, and as the creation of a saint, these coins are some of the most popular collector's items of this era.

These coins, created by a saint, are among the most popular of the era.

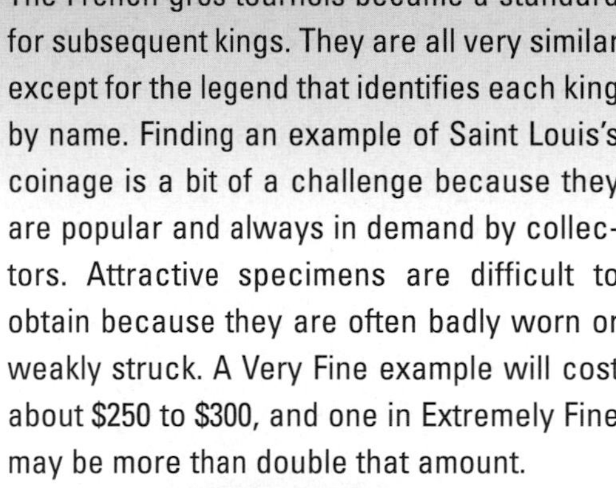

The French gros tournois became a standard for subsequent kings. They are all very similar except for the legend that identifies each king by name. Finding an example of Saint Louis's coinage is a bit of a challenge because they are popular and always in demand by collectors. Attractive specimens are difficult to obtain because they are often badly worn or weakly struck. A Very Fine example will cost about $250 to $300, and one in Extremely Fine may be more than double that amount.

2.4x actual size

Richard the Lionhearted

England. Richard I. Silver Obol. 1189–1199

King Richard I of England is perhaps best known today for his colorful epithet. This is not to say that he was not an important character in history, but many of his real deeds have been overshadowed by romantic legends that have sprung up concerning his somewhat vague lifestyle, as portrayed in stories about his exploits with the mythical Robin Hood. Historically, he was a larger-than-life figure. As a brave and fierce fighter, he sometimes foolhardily charged into battle with little armor. It is said that he also had a fiery temper that, as much as his bravery, earned him the "Lionhearted" nickname.

English silver pennies of Richard (top) and John (bottom). (1.5x actual size)

Richard was the eldest son of King Henry II and Eleanor of Aquitaine. He became king upon his father's death in 1189, and quickly realized his great ambition: to lead the Crusade to recapture Jerusalem from the Muslims. His character as a knight and his prowess in leading the Third Crusade (1189–1192) made Richard an admired king in his own time, as well as a legendary hero. Although brilliant in battle, he never did take Jerusalem, and he was forced to begin a return trip to England to reassert his kingship after his long absence.

After Richard left the Crusades for England in 1192, he was seized by political enemies in Austria and handed over to Henry VI, the Holy Roman Emperor. The emperor ransomed Richard for 1,500,000 marks—money that had to be raised from the English people. According to legend Richard's greatest supporter in England was Robin Hood, a bandit who took the money from the rich supporters of the king's brother Prince John, who was hoping to seize the throne for himself. Richard was released in 1194, but he never returned to England. Embroiled in wars in France, he was struck by a crossbow bolt in 1199 and died a few days later.

Richard's only coins with his name were issued in western France for his provinces in Aquitaine, Poitou, and Normandy. These were small silver deniers or obols of rather debased metal. In England he made silver pennies of the type and name of his father, Henry II. These are nearly identical to the coins of Henry and, later, the coins of Prince John, who succeeded Richard and ruled as king from 1199 to 1216. None of Richard's coins that were made in France have his portrait, but they do show his name together with that of the city where they were issued.

Admirers of Richard *Coeur de Lion* find his coins intriguing not only for his unusual name and fame as a Crusader, but also because of his identification in popular stories about Robin Hood and his Merry Men. Theirs was a gallant battle to restore the throne to its rightful occupant, and prevent Richard's evil brother John from seizing power.

Obols of Richard I from Poitou and Aquitaine are plentiful but always in demand. Extremely Fine pieces are definitely exceptional, but nice Very Fine coins can usually be found for $100 to $125.

3.53x actual size

The Great Genghis Khan

MONGOL TRIBES. GENGHIS KHAN. BILLON DIRHEM. 1220–1221

There is little doubt that Genghis Khan earned his place in history through extensive conquests. One would enjoy seeing his likeness on a coin, or even having something readily available to mark this numismatic record, but that is not the way it is. His coin types are few, and all are scarce. None of them are noted for their aesthetic value, and most are poorly struck. Furthermore, his coins are difficult to identify, and somewhat uninteresting for most collectors. Consequently, they are not valued commensurate with their actual scarcity, and seem like real bargains.

Genghis Khan, whose birth name was Temujin, was the eldest son of Yesugai, chief of the Borjigid clan of the Mongols. He spent his youth in the wilderness, and slowly built a rapport with all of the Mongol tribes, who acknowledged his leadership in 1206. At that time, he was given the title *Genghis Khan* (Very Mighty King) and proclaimed "Khan of Khans." His first conquests were in northern China, where he captured the capital of Chung-tu (Beijing) in 1214. When the growing expansion of the Mongol empire came to the attention of the Muslim world, an embassy from Persia was sent to the Great Khan offering peaceful relationships and trade agreements.

This initial accord was soon destroyed by a renegade tribe of Persians who intercepted a caravan of Mongol traders, murdered them, and stole their possessions. In retaliation, in 1219 the Mongol forces engaged the Persians, and seeing their weakened defenses, went forward to conquer the entire Persian empire. They then continued westward, overcoming forces in Russia, Hungary, and Poland. When Genghis died in 1227, the Mongol realm extended from the Black Sea to China, and encompassed much of Russia, Afghanistan, Turkistan, and Persia.

Mongol influence in the subjugated countries was widespread and included many cultural achievements. Genghis showed an abiding appreciation of all things artistic, and encouraged changes and innovations. Subsequent rulers of the Mongol empire continued his programs of expanding artistic modes and culture through the realm, and made significant impact on the history of the world.

Coin types of Genghis Khan are few, and all are scarce.

The base-silver dirhem shown here has no date, but was likely struck sometime around 1221, and was possibly made in Afghanistan by the conquering Khan. It is one of his most readily available coins, and pieces are usually priced from $75 to $150 in Very Fine condition. Gold pieces with his name are occasionally offered in Fine condition at prices from $2,500 to $3,000. Most are weakly struck with portions of the legend missing and are difficult to identify. Similar gold pieces of the later Mongol khans are much more common and are often available for about $200.

3.53x actual size

Christianity Flourishes in Ethiopia

AXUM. NEZOUA. GOLD 1/3 SOLIDUS (?). CIRCA 450 A.D.

While Ethiopia is somewhat removed from the medieval epoch of Europe, its history is so closely interrelated that it must be cited for the impact it had on the events of that time and its unique contributions to this episode. Although few enthusiasts consider coins of medieval Ethiopia to be high on their list of favorites, those who know about the many unique features of this nation, and its unusual money, are keen to have at least one representative specimen. They serve to illustrate this land's very unique traditions and culture.

Axum was the only autonomous state besides Persia and Rome to issue gold portrait coins.

In ancient times the area now known as Ethiopia consisted mainly of a small kingdom called Axum (or Aksum) that was located on the Red Sea. It was an important trading center from early times because of its location on the route linking India and southern Arabia with Rome by way of Egypt. Trade flourished between Egypt, Persia, India, Arabia, Rome, and Byzantium. Business conducted by Axum merchants not only made the area wealthy, but also presented an incentive for the district to coin its own money at a time when no other sub-Saharan African state had done so. The coins that it issued from around A.D. 270 to 740 are some of the only remaining records of the monarchs of that era. They are also exceptional in that Axum was the only other autonomous state besides Persia and Rome to issue gold portrait coins.

The unique features of Axum money are not the only reasons that collectors are drawn to this facet of history. The region boasts a very early evolution that goes back to the time of "Lucy," who is believed to be the oldest discovered hominid ancestor, and may have lived in this area 3.5 million years ago. The early history of Ethiopia as a nation is a mixture of fact and fiction that includes a colorful chapter that is included in a biblical account in First Kings. There it is told how in the 10th century B.C., Makeda, the queen of Sheba, journeyed from Ethiopia to Jerusalem to visit King Solomon. She reportedly brought with her "a very great train, with camels that had spices, gold, and precious stones."

The queen was greeted warmly by Solomon, who gave her great gifts, and impressed her with his wisdom. Upon her return home she vowed to adopt the God of Israel as her own. Her time with Solomon also produced a son, Menelik, who in time founded the line of the Lion of Judah, and became the first recognized Ethiopian king. Like his mother, he traveled to the Holy Land, and one account says that he removed the Ark of the Covenant, to protect it from destruction at the hands of the Babylonians, and carried it to Axum where it remains today, hidden somewhere within the walls of the city. Some say it is now concealed in or near the Ethiopian Orthodox Church of Our Lady Mary of Zion. Replicas of the Ark can be seen in churches throughout Ethiopia, together with copies of the Tablets of Moses, but the secret hiding place of the true Ark has remained undisclosed throughout the centuries.

3.33x actual size

In the second century A.D., the Axumite kingdom grew to be strong and powerful, with boundaries that extended beyond Ethiopia and into Arabia. Its merchants were known far and wide, and their port of Adulis on the Red Sea became an international trading center. During the reign of Ezanas from 330 to 370, this most famous and important Axumite king was introduced to Christianity by Frumentius, the bishop of Axum, from the Coptic Church of Alexandria in Egypt. Ezanas was converted to Christianity shortly thereafter, and Axum became the religious capital of the Ethiopian Orthodox Church. At this point, probably sometime near the year 332 A.D., Christianity was made their official state religion, making Axum the second ancient state, after Armenia, to adopt Christianity. The faith then spread throughout the Roman Empire and to the rest of the world.

The once-powerful Axumite kingdom began to decline during the seventh century, and lost control of Arabia, which was conquered by the Sassanian Persians. It was soon surrounded by Islamic states, and when Egypt fell to Islam in 640 A.D. Axum was cut off from Byzantium and Mediterranean ports. As a state, Ethiopia managed to coexist peacefully with its neighbors, but with extensive trade cut off, its need for a local currency ended during the eighth century.

Coin designs that were used throughout this series are apt to seem monotonous and repetitious. They consist mostly of unrecognizable heads, crosses, and the occasional seated figure. The generally worn condition, plus difficult-to-read inscriptions, leaves these coins rather unappreciated by most collectors. They should not be overlooked, because they fill a niche in the numismatic history of the world—unparalleled by any other type of coin.

The earliest Axumite coins were gold pieces approximately equal to one-third of the Roman solidus. They are uniform in design with an image of the monarch on each side, and symbols of the sun and crescent moon. With the advent of Christianity, the design was changed slightly to include a cross above the head. Very small gold coins were also made prior to 330 A.D., with a head on the obverse and a simple legend on the reverse. The tiny gold pieces are extremely rare and valued above $600. A one-third solidus of Exanas may cost up to $1,000. The condition of all gold coins is usually Very Fine to Extremely Fine. • Gold pieces of the revised Christian type are somewhat more common than the earlier coins. Nice specimens are generally available at prices ranging from $400 to $1,000. The bronze coins that were made during this period are far rarer than gold. They too show the head of the reigning monarch on the obverse, but usually show a cross and legend on the reverse. On some of the bronze pieces the cross is decorated with gold that was applied during the minting process. A few of the bronze coins show a seated figure of the king rather than a bust. Bronze coins of Axum are scarce, and most show signs of excessive wear. Fine specimens are generally valued at $75 to $200. All silver coins are decidedly scarce and the most valuable of all. Very Fine specimens sell quickly for $500 and more. • The bronze coins with a gold inlay on the reverse are some of the most unusual of all ancient coins. The process seems to have been a unique innovation intended to add value to the coins and make them distinctive. The "key" coins of China, made in the first century A.D., are the only other similar instances of such a feature.

Axum bronze coin of Kaleb(circa 525) with gold inlay on reverse. (1.5x actual size)

Bronze coin (eighth century) of Armah, showing the king seated and holding a cross. The cross on the reverse was inlaid with a fleck of gold—often missing, as it is on this specimen. (1.5x actual size)

An Artistic Achievement

Naples. Charles II d'Anjou. Silver Carlino. 1285–1309

Medieval coinage is noted for its many contrasts in styles and artistry. Some of the coins of this period are bland in design, crudely made, or devoid of artistic quality. Others seem way ahead of their time in innovation and excellence. Those most popular with collectors either display unusual artistic merit or are of special historical significance.

The scene on this popular coin is of the Annunciation to the Virgin Mary of the impending birth of her son.

In the case of the coin shown here it is the design, rather than any great historical relevance, that collectors find to be significant and attractive. The famous scene depicts the Annunciation to the Virgin Mary of the impending birth of her son Jesus. In this rendering, the archangel Gabriel is shown standing on the left, pointing a finger at Mary, who is standing at the right. There are lilies in a vase between them. On the reverse is the ducal coat of arms of Jerusalem and Anjou.

Coins of this design were struck in both silver and gold sometime around the year 1300, at a time when artistry of this caliber was rarely seen elsewhere. These pieces are popularly known as *saluto d'argento, saluto d'oro*, or simply *saluto* because of the design, and are perennial favorites with collectors. The silver carlino is the most readily available piece; gold examples are slightly more difficult to locate and are priced somewhat higher.

Charles I, king of Naples and Sicily (1266 to 1285) and count of Anjou and Provence, was the youngest brother of King Louis IX of France. He took part in Louis's crusades to Egypt and Tunisia, and later ruled over parts of France, Poland, and Hungary. Upon his death in 1285, his son Charles II became king of Naples and count of Anjou and Provence. Known as "Charles the Lame," he had been captured by Roger of Lauria in the naval battle at Naples in 1284, and was still a prisoner of Peter III of Aragon when he assumed the crown. In 1288 King Edward I of England mediated his release, and Charles was liberated and allowed to return to Naples.

Throughout his turbulent reign, Charles gave up all of his rights to Sicily, and he spent the last years of his life in Naples, where he made many enhancements. He died in 1309 and was succeeded by his son Robert the Wise. It was during this time that Venice introduced its gold coin known as a *ducat* (in 1284); Arnolfo di Cambio designed the cathedral of Florence (in 1297); and while being held in a Genoese jail in 1298, Marco Polo wrote the incredible story of his travels throughout Asia. In 1300, near the time that this coin was made, the last Muslims in Sicily were forcibly converted to Christianity.

Silver carlinos of Charles II are priced at around $250 for Extremely Fine examples. His gold pieces are somewhat more expensive and much scarcer. They sell for $1,000 or more for choice pieces. The design is the same on both denominations, and either will make a delightful artistic addition to any collection of medieval coinage.

2.5x actual size

A Saintly Pursuit

Merovingian Kingdom. Dagobert I. Gold Tremissis. 629–639

No collection of popular medieval coins would be complete without including an example of those made by the only moneyer who was declared a saint of the Church. This fascinating person, who is known to us as Bishop Eligius, or Saint Eloi, was at one time goldsmith to the Frankish king Dagobert I. When Bishop Eligius died, he was proclaimed saint and patron of all workers in metal.

The Merovingians were a dynasty of Frankish kings who ruled in parts of present-day France and Germany from the fifth to the eighth century. Their claim to sovereignty was based on mythical "divine descent" and military success. Stories of their lineage have recently been exploited by the authors of *Holy Blood, Holy Grail* and *The DaVinci Code*. In those accounts the hypothesis is that Jesus' supposed marriage to Mary Magdalene produced descendants who intermarried with the Merovingians, giving that line of kings their divine authority.

Constant squabbling between the various Merovingian rulers of the sixth and seventh centuries resulted in a diminished kingdom and lessening of their powers. This changed in 629 when Dagobert I became king and successor to his father, Clotaire II. Under Dagobert's rule, the Merovingian monarchy attained its highest point of importance and influence. He restored control over lands that had been taken by nobles and by the Church. He was also a patron of the arts. His delight in things exquisite was promoted through the craftsmanship of his treasurer, the goldsmith Eligius. Dagobert also positioned qualified prelates in the bishoprics, with Eligius (Eloi) filling the important seat at Noyon shortly after the king's death. His reign as bishop is remembered for the building of several monasteries and renewed missionary activity in Flanders.

King Dagobert has been immortalized in the song "Le Bon Roi Dagobert" (The Good King Dagobert), a nursery rhyme about the adventures of the king and his advisor, Saint Eligius. On the death of Dagobert in 639, Eligius left the court and entered the priesthood, where he undertook the conversion of the Flemings and other pagan tribes. He died peacefully in his bishopric of Noyon in 660, and is still venerated in Antwerp, Flanders, and other places as the patron saint of goldsmiths, blacksmiths, and coin collectors. His feast day on the Roman Catholic calendar is December 1, a day that is set aside to honor his memory and the efforts of all who work in numismatics.

During his time as goldsmith to Dagobert, Eligius designed and minted gold coins for the king. Some of these show his name as minter, and as such, they are particular favorites among collectors who treasure them as relics of this great saint.

Eligius, the patron saint of those who work in numismatics, was the goldsmith to Good King Dagobert.

All Merovingian gold coins are scarce or rare. They are valued around $2,500 for any available pieces. Those made by St. Eloi are particular favorites among collectors and, while seldom available, are worth $3,000 or more.

5.45x actual size

CHAPTER 5

The World of Islam

Foes of the Crusaders

Turkomans in Syria. Hussaneddin Yuluk-Arslan. Bronze Dirham. A.H. 580–597 (A.D. 1184–1201)

Islamic coinage extends over nearly 14 centuries, and encompasses a region from Spain and Morocco in the west to Malaya and Indonesia in the east. Early Islamic coinage was mostly imitative of local issues familiar to regions that had been conquered. A purer Islamic coinage began when the empire expanded its influence in the seventh century. The sphere of Islamic influence throughout its formative years is difficult to follow, and fraught with inconsistencies, wars, and frequent turmoil. The rapidly expanding influence of Islam led to concern and resentment among Christians, in particular throughout the Byzantine Empire.

While the fortunes of war fluctuated, coins were produced that typified the battling forces.

The immediate cause of the First Crusade is rather clouded. In 1009 the Fatimid caliph al-Hakim bi-Amr Allah sacked the pilgrimage hospice in Jerusalem and destroyed the Church of the Holy Sepulcher. Pilgrims were frequently aggravated or robbed, and Byzantine emperors began appealing to the pope for protection and guidance. Hostilities between the Seljuk Turks and Christians escalated through the 11th century and culminated in 1095 with the beginning of the Crusades.

While the fortunes of war fluctuated over the following 200 years, numerous coins were produced that typify the battling forces. Among the most remarkable are those known as Turkoman figural bronze issues. The distinctive designs on these coins are unique in that they portray both human and animal figures to a degree unlike any other Islamic coins. Some of the designs are clearly copied from ancient coins of several cultures earlier; some likely represent symbolic Christian concepts. All challenge the imagination to interpret what the creators intended.

With more than a hundred designs to choose from, at least one of the Turkoman figural bronzes should be included in any representative collection of this period of history. A particular favorite of many numismatists is the one shown here. It is an Artuqid bronze dirham of Hussaneddin Yuluk-Arslan, who ruled in A.H. 580 to 597 (A.D. 1184–1201). The design has been explained as representing the mourning of the death in A.H. 589 (A.D. 1193) of the great Muslim defender Saladin. It was he who led their triumphant armies against the infidel Franks, and the weeping attendants were a fitting design for commemoration of the death of this famous Saracen leader.

Turkoman figural bronzes are relatively common, but nearly always are available only in worn or corroded condition. It is frequently difficult to read the inscriptions and dates, but the basic designs are usually quite evident. Any one of several good references will be necessary to catalog these pieces, but the challenge is well worth the effort. A piece in Fine to Very Fine condition for $125 is about as nice as will be found, and there is very little difference in value for most of the designs.

2.07x actual size

The Great Saladin

Turkomans in Syria. Hussaneddin Yuluk-Arslan. Bronze Dirham. A.H. 584 (A.D. 1188)

The first noteworthy Ayyubid sultan was the great Saladin, who ruled from A.H. 564 to 589 (A.D. 1169 to 1193). Born in 1137 of Kurdish descent, he spent much of his youth in Damascus where he distinguished himself by his interest in Sunni theology. By age 30 he had participated in campaigns against the Fatimid rulers of Egypt, and eventually became vizier (high-ranking political advisor) there. In time, he succeeded in subduing the Shiite Fatimid caliph, and proclaimed himself sultan of all Egypt in 1171, thus beginning the Ayyubid dynasty.

Saladin's conquests continued at a rapid pace, and he soon advanced westward on the northern shores of Africa to Qabis and on to Yemen. After taking over Damascus, he attempted to subdue all of Syria and Palestine. His campaigns brought him into conflict with the Christian crusaders in the Latin Orient, and in constant offenses against Jerusalem. Though unsuccessful in his efforts to conquer the Assassins in their mountain strongholds, he did come to treat them as allies, and he overcame Mosul, Aleppo, and other districts controlled by rival Muslim rulers. By 1180, he had become the undisputed leading Islamic warrior.

With his growing strength, Saladin set out to assault the Christians. He first attacked Raymond of Tripoli, a former ally who had joined with other Crusaders at the battle of Hattin in 1187. Saladin not only won, but also captured Guy of Lusignan and Reginald of Chatillon. He also took the city of Jerusalem, igniting fervor for yet another Crusade.

When forces gathered for the Third Crusade in 1189, it was the English king Richard the Lionhearted who traveled to Jerusalem in an attempt to recover the Holy City. The two distinguished leaders thus met in a heroic conflict that has come to be remembered in lore and legend. The stories of Saladin's reputation for generosity and chivalry seem to be based in fact, and he admired Richard as a worthy opponent. This Crusade failed to recapture Jerusalem, but it did free Akka, and in 1192, the opposing forces came to an agreement with the Peace of Ramla that left the Latin Kingdom with only a small strip of land along the coast from Tyre to Yafo.

Ayyubid coins bearing the name of Saladin are rather scarce and difficult to identify. There are, however, a number of Turkoman bronze coins that were made under his control, and with his name. The first of these was made for the Artuqids of Mardin by Hussaneddin Yuluk-Arslan. The piece presented here is dated A.H. 584 (A.D. 1188), and may show a portrait of Saladin. Another popular bronze coin of this same ruler is one that, for no known reason, shows the bust of a Roman and Byzantine emperor.

Bronze Turkoman coin variety with two portraits. (Actual size)

Turkoman figural bronze coins issued in the name of Saladin are in constant demand and are generally priced at $150, or a bit higher than most other similar Turkoman pieces.

2.07x actual size

Our Coins or Yours?

Arab-Byzantine. Anonymous Bronze Fals. Circa A.D. 700
Latin Kingdom of Jerusalem. Gold Bezant. 1187–1250

Despite a continual enmity between Muslims and Christians, economic needs made it necessary for each to maintain a supply of usable money that would be acceptable in trade. To that end, concessions were often made in coinage designs to facilitate familiarity and circulation among people of differing customs.

Despite constant tension, Muslims and Christians needed common coins that could cross the boundaries of war.

When Mohammed died in 632, his followers gradually extended his influence throughout North Africa and into Spain. At its greatest expansion the Omayyad Caliphate embraced areas from southern France eastward to Afghanistan. The Omayyads adopted and adapted the Byzantine and Sassanian management of the provinces they conquered; they also attempted to produce coinage that would be acceptable to them. The first copper coins of the Muslims are the so-called Arab-Byzantine coins known as fulus, a word derived from the Latin word "follis."

There is some uncertainty about the exact date when these coins were produced, but they certainly must have been in circulation by the beginning of the eighth century. Many of them were struck at mints in North Africa, Palestine, Syria, and Damascus. The most common design imitates a bronze coin of the Byzantine emperor Heraclius (610–641) who successfully defeated the Persian and Sassanian armies in 622, and shows a standing Byzantine emperor on the obverse, and the letter M surmounted by a cross on the reverse. A second design, as on the coin illustrated here, shows a standing caliph on the obverse, and a pseudo-cross (an imitation of the Christian cross shown on many Byzantine coins) on the reverse. The legends on both of these designs are primarily in Arabic, with occasional Roman letters.

The second coin used here to illustrate this unusual period in history is a gold dinar or bezant of the Latin Kingdom of Jerusalem. It was made around 1200, during the Islamic occupation, and imitates the familiar coins of Caliph al-Amir. The legends, which are in pseudo-Kufic, imitating Arabic words, are sometimes unintelligible, or contained decidedly Christian sentiment. Although these designs were made and used out of necessity, they were resented by Christians and were gradually changed to include crosses and strict Christian legends. In the end, these coins were unacceptable to both Christians and Muslims and soon became obsolete.

Arab-Byzantine anonymous bronze fulus of the eighth century are relatively common and generally priced at about $50 for pieces in Fine to Very Fine condition. There seems to be little difference in the value of those with the Byzantine emperor and those with the (more interesting) Islamic caliph. They are often worn or poorly made, and rarely found in high grade. • Gold bezants of Latin Jerusalem are in constant demand and are well worth the $800 to $1,000 that one will cost in Very Fine or better condition. Those that show a cross as part of the design are somewhat more desirable, and will likely be priced somewhat above $1,000. Average condition is Very Fine to Extremely Fine.

2.25 and 2.05x actual size

A Numismatic Love Story

Seljuks of Rum. Kay-Khusrau II. Silver Dirhem. 1243–1244

One of the most attractive, unusual, and interesting coins struck by the Seljuks of Rum is the "lion and sun" dirhem. It is uncharacteristic of a Muslim coin type because it is representational rather than being composed entirely of Arabic script. Not that this is a unique feature (it is frequently seen in Turkoman coins of the same period), but figural designs are rarely seen throughout most Muslim coinage because of religious constraints. In this case the design is a touching reminder of a love story between a Muslim ruler and a Christian princess.

The Seljuks of Rum were one of the subdivisions of Turks who ruled all of western Asia from Afghanistan to the border of the Greek Empire in Asia Minor, as well as the Fatimid Caliphate of Egypt. In 1071 they had defeated the Byzantine army and stopped the crusaders. By 1078, they had reached as far as Nicaea, near Constantinople, where they ruled for the next two centuries.

Kay-Khusrau II was the son of Sultan Kayqobad I and a Greek princess. He ruled from A.H. 634 to 643 (A.D. 1237 to 1245). During his father's reign and the beginning of his own, the Seljuks of Rum were at the height of their military power and territorial expansion. An alliance with Aleppo had been sealed in 1232 when Kay-Khusrau, still a prince, had married the daughter of the Eyyubite ruler of Aleppo.

Soon after his forced marriage, he fell passionately in love with and married the daughter of Queen Tamara of Georgia. Kay-Khusrau treated the lovely princess Russudana in all respects as his lawful wife, and she became known to the Seljuks as Goorgei Khatun (the Georgian Queen). While the union had all the marks of a true love affair, it also served to protect the northeastern boundaries of the kingdom.

Kay-Khusru had originally asked his father for a Latin princess as a bride, and promised that she could keep her religion and maintain an entire Christian household. He said that he would build churches in all his cities and pay Christian priests to officiate in them. He even hinted that if his bride should prove to be truly affectionate he might himself adopt Christianity.

This coin is a touching reminder of a love story between a Muslim ruler and a Christian princess.

Considering the role of women of that time and place, it is remarkable that Russudana came to exercise such influence on the sultan. It is said that when he married her, he was so much in love that he wanted to include her portrait beside his own on his coins. This radical departure from tradition was too drastic for his viziers, and he was advised to give up the idea and not even to include her name with his on the coins. The sultan, however, was not to be dissuaded and he conceived a bold plan to achieve his goal.

Instead of issuing coins with the two portraits, he used a unique design showing a lion on the obverse, representing himself, and a blazing sun above, representing Russudana's radiance. It was a magnificent tribute to his beloved wife, and an act of love unparalleled in numismatic history. The "lion and sun" coins

2.86x actual size

of Kay-Khusrau were struck at several mints during a three-year period from A.H. 638 to 640 (A.D. 1240 to 1243). A number of different varieties exist that differ in the details on the obverse, and the arrangement of the legends on the reverse.

It would be pleasant if a love story of this extent would have ended with "and they lived happily ever after," but that was not the case. Around the time these coins were made, an insurrection broke out pitting Seljuk city dwellers against the Turcoman nomad tribes of the Anatolia. Under Baba Ishaq and other dervish leaders, a growing resentment arose over the form and customs of Islam that should be observed. The marriage of Kay-Khusrau to a Christian was an affront not to be taken lightly. It was even rumored that Kay-Khusrau had secretly embraced Christianity. Hostilities flared up, with the city workers and the nomads (in this case the Greek and Armenian artisans ruled by the Seljuk Turks) opposing the Turkoman tribes of Anatolia who clung to their own form of popular Islam.

After two years of fighting, Baba Ishaq was defeated with the help of Latin mercenaries, but the Seljuks were so weakened from the long struggle that Mongol raiders penetrated their frontiers, and soon took over much of the territory. Kay-Khusru abandoned everything and fled to Adalia and from there to the Greek border. His mother and daughter took refuge at the court of the Armenia ruler Hetum I. There they stayed until Hetum acceded to a demand to deliver them to the Mongols. In 1245–1246 Seljuk troops reentered Armenia with the help of the Armenian baron, Constantine II, in a revolt against Hetum. They were only able to seize a few forts, which the Mongols later forced them to abandon. As a result of the Mongol invasion, there was general ineptitude among the Seljuks, and, during a revolt, a group of ranking officials strangled Kay-Khusrau. As for Russudana, she soon followed the prevailing custom for widows of rulers, and married another noble with whom she lived for the remainder of her life.

Bilingual silver trams with the inscriptions of Armenian king Hetum I and Kay-Khusru I, struck at Sis (1204–1210). (Actual size)

Typical Turkoman bronze coin of Nasir al-Din Artuq Arslan (1201–1239). Struck at Mardin in 606 A.H. (Actual size)

Silver dirhems of Kay-Khusrau II are not particularly rare, and are frequently available in Very Fine to Extremely Fine condition. Their unusual and attractive design makes them a prime target for collectors. Prices generally run from $90 to $150 depending on how well struck and complete they are. Heavily worn specimens are rather unattractive, and many are clipped or missing portions of the reverse inscription.

Silver dirhem of Kay-Khusru II, with alternate reverse. (2x actual size)

Coins of the Slave Kings

Mamluk Coinage. Al Ashraf Shaban II. Bronze Fals. 1363–1377

The Mamluks were originally slaves who had been captured by Abbasid caliphs in areas north of the Black Sea, or who had been kidnapped by slave-traders. In time, many of them converted to Islam, and were trained as cavalry soldiers. They were well known for their horsemanship, archery, and loyalty to their overlords; soon they became indispensable to the sultan. Many of the more ambitious Mamluk slaves were able to gain high positions throughout the empire, including army commands. At first their status remained non-hereditary and sons were not allowed to follow their fathers, but that changed in places such as Egypt, where many gained significant power and influence.

After the death of Saladin his empire fell into disarray and the Ayyubids became increasingly surrounded by the powerful Mamluks who had become involved in the internal court politics of the kingdom itself. When the Mongol troops of Hulegu Khan sacked Baghdad and took over Damascus in 1258, one of those who escaped was the Mamluk general Baibars. He fled to Cairo, and mobilized his troops there. The Mamluks eventually defeated the Mongols in 1260 and began to consolidate their power. Baibars's troops also defeated the last of the Crusader states in the Holy Land.

The Mamluks quickly grew in power and soon developed into a major dynasty, with their capital in Cairo. Among the many achievements of the Mamluk period, from 1250 to 1350, was their historical recording, better standards of living, good relations with foreign powers, and peaceful relations between peoples inside the state. Their greatest weakness was not establishing clear lines of succession to the throne, and very few of the emperors died of natural causes.

The story of the Mamluk rise from slaves to masters is one that surely has a poignant moral. The Abbasid Empire grew weak from near-total dependence on slaves, who were placed in control of everything from the army to affairs of state. The exchange of power inevitably led to the logical conclusion where slave and master changed roles, and the victors became the vanquished. By giving up responsibility for control of their lives, the Abbasids also gave up their claim to freedom.

The story of the Mamluk rise from slaves to masters has a poignant moral.

Mamluk coinage consisted of gold, silver, and bronze, and is unusual in the many variations of size, weight, and fineness that occur over a relatively short span of time. A majority of the pieces are similar in style to other Islamic coins of that time, with formulaic legends and few other features. Some contain a small unexplained lion or other ornaments, but are without human representations.

Bronze fals are plentiful and are of interest to collectors for their heraldic devices, as well as their connection to the slave kings of Egypt. When located, they usually sell for prices from $20 to $25, but the challenge is to find one that is in legible condition and properly identified. Silver pieces are worth between $50 and $100. Gold examples are rare.

3x actual size

Tales of the Arabian Nights

Abbasids. Harun al Rashid. Silver Dirhem. A.D. 785–809

The Abbasid sultan Schahriar had a wife whom he loved more than all the world. He showered her with gifts and all that could bring her happiness, but one day to his great sorrow he learned that she had been unfaithful. Obliged to carry out the law of the land, he ordered the grand vizier to put her to death. In his troubled state, the sultan believed that all women were probably wicked and the world would be better without them. Thereafter, every evening he married a new wife, and had her strangled the following morning.

The brilliant Scheherazade conceived a plan to free the kingdom of the sultan's reign of terror. . . .

It was the duty of the grand vizier to select the ill-fated wives for the sultan. Being the father of two daughters, he was greatly distressed in knowing that their turn would eventually be at hand. The grand vizier's eldest daughter was named Scheherazade, and the younger was Dinarzade. Of the two, Scheherazade was the most talented, having been schooled in philosophy, medicine, history, and fine arts. She was also reputed to be the most beautiful girl in the entire kingdom of Persia.

The brilliant Scheherazade conceived a plan to free the kingdom of the sultan's barbaric reign of terror and asked her father to propose that she become the sultan's bride. With great reluctance he agreed, and when she was delivered she only asked that her sister be allowed to stay with her on her last night. At a prearranged time Dinarzade asked if Scheherazade would tell one of her fascinating stories, and the sultan agreed to allow this. At a time when there were no printed books, the tale she told was enthralling, and so she began telling the first of what became 1,001 stories of the Arabian nights. So engrossing were the nightly tales that they broke the sultan's horrible routine, and he never took another wife for the rest of his life.

Many of Scheherazade's stories involved local personalities and events familiar to those times. A number of them focused on Sinbad the Sailor, and most were set in the time of the great caliph, Harun al Rashid, who ruled in Baghdad from A.D. 785 to 809. Legend holds that it was he who actually was the caliph responsible for this tragic legend.

While the tales Scheherazade told of 1,001 Arabian nights may be fables, Harun al Rashid was a real person and one of the most famous Abbasid caliphs. He is still remembered for his stunning defeat of the Byzantine emperor Nicephorus I, and through his extensive coinage of silver dirhems. The usual design on his coins has a complex Kufic legend that proclaims, "There is no God but God alone and Mohammed is the Prophet of God."

A Very Fine silver dirhem of Harun al Rashid will cost from $150 to $200. Lesser-condition pieces are sometimes seen at lower prices, but they are rather unattractive. Some of his coins do not contain his name, but can be identified by the date or magistrate's name that is usually included.

2.61x actual size

The Fire Worshipers

SASSANIAN KINGDOM. KHUSRO II. SILVER DRACHM. A.D. 591–628

Coins of the Arab-Sassanian Kingdom are notable for their unusual depiction of fire worshipers as the design on the reverse. Despite many other Sassanian claims to fame, collector interest in these pieces is often focused on the religious aspects of their ancient customs. On the obverse of these oversized and impressive silver drachms is the profile head of the reigning monarch, wearing a large crown or imposing headdress. The reverse depicts a fire altar flanked by two attendants. Symbols of the sun and moon are sometimes shown, while various dates and Arabic inscriptions complete the design.

The origin of the Zoroastrian religion that is represented by the fire and attendants shown on these coins is unknown, but it may have had its beginnings in very ancient times. It is one of only a few monotheistic religions, and took its name from the prophet Zoroaster, who lived sometime around 600 B.C. It was a prominent faith throughout Persia until crushed by the conquests of Alexander the Great. It again arose as an important religion for the Sassanians in A.D. 226. With the rapid spread of Islam around 630, the Zorastrians again faced persecution and many converted to Islam under fear of death. Arab-Sassanian coins showing the fire-worshipping scene are a significant reminder of this chapter in history, which has been overlooked in many other chronicles, and a link to the past for an ancient religion that exists today in only a few isolated places.

The Zoroastrians did not actually worship fire as an idol. The religious system taught a devotion to Ormazd (the Creator) in the context of a universal struggle between the forces of light and darkness. Fire was a sacred symbol for the Zoroastrians, who kept it burning in respect for their priests, warriors, and farmers. Fire was ranked according to its many uses by artisans, through cooking and hearth fires, up to the great eternal flame that was kept burning in places of worship.

Khusro II, who issued the coin shown here, was named "the Victorious," because of his victories over Byzantine armies in their many struggles for power. He won remarkable battles at Damascus in 613, and then at Jerusalem and Alexandria in 619. However, the Byzantine armies fought back, and under the leadership of Heraclius, Khusro's own palace was destroyed in 627. Khusro died while the empire was in revolt the following year.

These coins are a significant link to an ancient religion that exists today in only a few places.

Silver drachms of Khusro II are relatively common, and nice specimens in Very Fine condition or better can usually be obtained for prices from $30 to $50. They were coined at several different mints, but collectors seem to be content to own representative pieces that clearly show the fire worshipers, regardless of issuer or mint. All of the coins in this series have the same basic design. Some of the many different issues by various kings are rare and valuable.

1.88x actual size

An Extraordinary Misunderstanding

Kashmir. Ranbir Singh. Silver Rupee. A.D. 1860

We all make mistakes. Some are just more discomforting than others. Some mistakes are forgotten with time, while a few of them are emblazoned where everyone can see them forever. Such was the fate of a misunderstanding that became part of a coin design and is now permanently recorded in numismatic history.

The incident occurred many years ago in Kashmir, a tiny province in northern India that was part of Afghanistan until 1811. It remained under Afghan sway until 1819, when it was conquered by the Sikhs. From then on, Kashmir was ruled by a succession of governors appointed by the maharajas of the Punjab, until the conquest by the British in 1845. The first raja under British rule was Gulab Singe, who paid a sum of £750,000 for the rights to the territory. His son, Raja Ranbir Singh, succeeded him and ruled from 1857 to 1885. It was the unfortunate Raja Ranbir Singh whose abiding claim to fame was a misguided coin design.

The unfortunate Raja Ranbir Singh's abiding claim to fame was a misguided coin design.

The coins in this incident were made by the raja from about 1857 to 1875, and they are conspicuous because of the letters JHS inscribed on them. The abbreviation is usually intended to represent *Jesus Hominum Salvator*, "Jesus Savior of Men," but in this case it was used by a profoundly religious Hindu ruler. Raja Ranbir Singh was known as a social reformer and was supportive of scholarship in Buddhist and Islamic texts, as well as his own faith, but was not well acquainted with Christianity, nor sympathetic to its beliefs.

Early in his reign, the raja made contact with Sir Henry Montgomery Lawrence, the British resident (colonial official). It was probably an uncomfortable meeting because Ranbir Singh held no love for the British and aspired to rid the country of them. At the meeting he asked Sir Henry, "Why is it that in the end the English always conquer, even though at first all goes against them?" Lawrence, who was apparently preoccupied, simply took a piece of paper, wrote the letters JHS, and handed it to the raja.

After pondering the letters, Ranbir Singh decided that they must be some form of magic formula or talisman that brought power and victory to those who use them. With a desire for emulating the British success, he immediately had the magic letters added to all of his coins in the belief that they would ensure victory in all of his undertakings.

The raja, who ruled for 38 years, effected a number of major improvements throughout his kingdom, including introduction of the native postal system in 1866. The area has long been renowned for the manufacture of superb silk products, carpets, and cashmere shawls. Perhaps in the end, the magic formula really did work in some unexplained way.

Silver and bronze coins of Kashmir showing the JHS letters are not particularly scarce. Extremely Fine specimens sell for prices under $50. Gold pieces are rarely encountered, and valued at about $2,500. They are all easily identified by the Roman letters JHS, while the rest of the inscription is in Arabic.

2.5x actual size

Glass Coins of Egypt

Egypt. Fatimid Caliphs. Glass Token. Circa A.D. 900

There is a long-held belief that glass coins were once used as money in Egypt. This conviction comes from evidence in the form of numerous coin-like objects that have defied a clear understanding of their nature and use. No one is even certain about when these intriguing artifacts were made, or why so many have survived. This is not to say that they are plentiful, but hundreds have been preserved and rest on the shelves of museums where they often remain unidentified and underappreciated.

For coin collectors these pieces are an enigma, only to be pondered when one occasionally appears on the market or in a dealer's stock. They look like coins in every respect, but they are definitely made of glass, and would have been undeniably impractical for long, hard usage as money. The inscriptions on these objects are always in Arabic and are often nearly impossible to decipher because of the weak or poor impressions in glass.

On the pleasing and intriguing side of this dilemma is the mystery and beauty of these fascinating pieces. They occur in a multitude of colors, shapes, and sizes, with seemingly endless variations in inscriptions. Their scarcity in the numismatic marketplace has made them almost legendary among collectors, who speak of them in muted or quizzical voices wondering about why and how these pieces were made.

Despite the intrigue and mystery surrounding these "glass coins of Egypt," they have not been totally unexplained or ignored by researchers. Also, they are not so expensive as to be out of the reach of would-be collectors. The greatest hindrance is locating a desirable specimen. The chase is well worth the effort because these striking pieces deserve a place in the numismatic history of the world.

Most students agree that there are three separate classes of these molded glass items. The first and most plentiful group is of weights. These are usually circular and flat with an impressed inscription on one side; the other side is blank. A second group consists of vessel stamps that were likely used to seal, safeguard, and identify the contents of ancient jars. These are similar to the weights but often have an irregular surface on the bottom side and are apt to be irregular in shape. They also have Arabic inscriptions embossed on the top side.

Pieces of the third category are by far the rarest and most desirable. They almost certainly are tokens, meant to have been used as a substitute for small change. They very closely resemble actual coins and have Arabic inscriptions on both sides. Like examples of the other groups, they are made of molded glass and occur with a variety of colors, sizes, and inscriptions. How, or why, these glass pieces ever functioned as money is a mystery we might never solve.

Egyptian glass weights, vessel stamps, and tokens were most likely made in the period from A.D. 700 to 900, although many other guesses have been proposed. Some speculate they may have continued in use

Fatimid glass seal (top) and glass weight (bottom). (Actual size)

2.22x actual size

as late as 1170. Others have even proposed that they were made hundreds of years earlier, but that is unlikely because of epigraphic evidence. They are attributed to the Umayyad and Abbasid cultures and were very likely common to many areas beyond Egypt.

It has been said that that the Umayyad caliph 'Abd al-Malik (684–707) first proposed that the testing of all coins should be carried out by using glass weights. His reasoning was that glass was not susceptible to alteration either by augmentation or diminution, because any tampering would be easily detected. He offered this suggestion as a remedy to the practice of passing coins that had been clipped and a portion of their metal removed. Clipping coins had been a means of minor thievery since ancient times, and one that continued until the use of mechanical production that added a decorated, reeded, or perfectly round edge to reveal any alteration.

These unusual items look like coins, but they are definitely made of glass.

We may never know for certain who was responsible for the introduction of glass weights, but the scenario must have been the same whenever they were first used. As a group, the weights seem to follow a pattern of being measured in units of dinar, dirham, and fals, all of which were equal to coin denominations. This close association with coins has been partially responsible for the wide-held belief that the weights themselves were actually coins or tokens.

Control of weights and measures was traditionally carried out under official supervision. Merchants were required to use only authorized, and carefully made, standard weights. Inspectors monitored such weights frequently and any that were found inaccurate were taken from the merchants, who were forced to buy others.

The stamps, or seals, which are similar in appearance to the weights and tokens, were very likely used to seal vessels and identify the contents or the seller. They very likely also served as a receipt for any taxes that might have been paid for the merchandise.

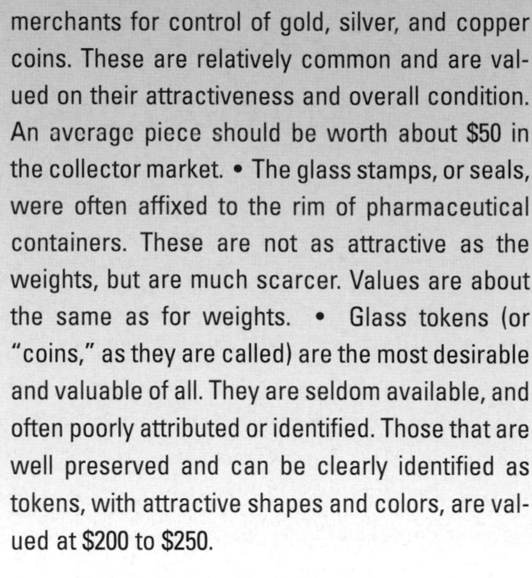
The weights may have been used by artisans and merchants for control of gold, silver, and copper coins. These are relatively common and are valued on their attractiveness and overall condition. An average piece should be worth about $50 in the collector market. • The glass stamps, or seals, were often affixed to the rim of pharmaceutical containers. These are not as attractive as the weights, but are much scarcer. Values are about the same as for weights. • Glass tokens (or "coins," as they are called) are the most desirable and valuable of all. They are seldom available, and often poorly attributed or identified. Those that are well preserved and can be clearly identified as tokens, with attractive shapes and colors, are valued at $200 to $250.

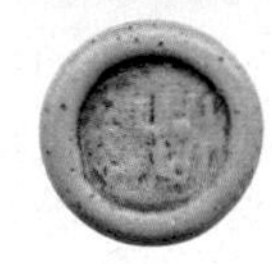

Glass seal (top) and glass weight (bottom). (Actual size)

Monnaie de Luxe

Ottoman Empire. Mahmud II ibn Abd al Hamid. Gold Double Altun. A.H. 1223 (A.D. 1808)

The French term *monnaie de luxe* may be unfamiliar to many coin collectors, but its meaning is exactly what one would expect. It refers to specially made coins that are elegant and luxurious. While this designation might describe most Proof coins, it is generally reserved to identify a certain kind of Turkish gold coin. The production of these unusual coins is a custom that goes back to the reign of Ahmet III (1703–1730), who originally had them made as special favors and presents for his friends.

A typical example is shown here to illustrate what most of the early monnaie de luxe coins look like. It is a nearly pure gold double altun of Mahmud II ibn Abd al Hamid. The value would have been considerable in 1808 (when this piece was made), and it must have been very happily accepted by the fortunate person who received it as a gift. (At least we can speculate that it was some sort of a gift.)

Legend says that these early pieces were traditionally given to women of the harem for their special favors. The exact role that these coins fulfilled is uncertain, but it is clear that many of them ended up being holed or looped so that they could be attached to clothing or a headband and used as jewelry. Wearing these coins in one way or another became a status symbol, a custom that has continued to the present, and various forms of the monnaie de luxe coins have continued to be made throughout the years to accommodate a constant demand for use as jewelry. They are also very popular with coin collectors and those who just want to invest in attractive and unusual gold coins. Modern versions are still being made in Turkey as a unique form of bullion coinage.

There are two distinguishing features that set these pieces apart from the gold coins that were made concurrently as normal circulating currency in the 18th and 19th centuries. Monnaie de luxe pieces are larger in diameter and thinner than ordinary Turkish gold coins. They are also made of a slightly lighter weight than corresponding denominations. The early pieces can easily be identified by their ornate designs and the large central toughra, or signature, which looks sort of like a scribbled fingerprint. That unusual design is actually a fancy way of writing the ruler's name, and it varies with each different issuer.

These very special "jewelry" coins have become so popular over the years that numerous base-metal imitations have been made for use as costume and decorative pieces. They often have the look and feel of antique coins, but are only gold-plated and have no numismatic value.

Legend says that these coins were given to women of the harem for their special favors.

Many of the early coins have been holed, but this does not seriously detract from their desirability. Some collectors appreciate them for their historical context, while others prefer unholed specimens. In general, the holed coins sell for about 20% less than undamaged pieces and vary in price according to size and age, but average about $300.

1.50x actual size

GEORGIVS·II·DEI·GRATIA·
LIMA

CHAPTER 6

Merry Olde England

Picasso Would Have Approved

Early Britain. Gallo-Belgic Gold Stater. Circa 60–55 B.C.

The first coins used in Britain were not local issues, but various pieces made in northeastern Gaul that came there through commercial channels. They were the so-called Gallo-Belgic coins that were typical of many Celtic coins used throughout Europe, and remarkable for their use of strange designs that seem reminiscent of devices that might have been drawn by the modern artist Pablo Picasso.

As a group, Celtic coins of that period are basically rough imitations of older coins from other cultures. Many of them copy the designs of ancient Macedonian gold or silver coins and often reproduce them in abstract forms. They sometimes seem to have been copied so many times the original design is barely recognizable. The most frequently copied are themes of coins of Philip II, which show what should be the head of Apollo on the obverse, and a horse, either with or without rider, on the reverse.

The Gallo-Belgic gold staters that were in use at the time that Julius Caesar invaded Britain are typical and popular examples of Celtic coins. This noteworthy piece shows a disjointed horse on one side, with scattered pellets and lines. The other side has purposely been left blank. It is made of good gold, but is considerably lighter in weight than the original stater of Macedonian king Philip II, made in the fourth century B.C., which it seems to imitate. The unusual representations used on these coins have never been fully explained; however, it seems certain that the designs were deliberately crafted and not simply degenerate work of unskilled artisans. These coins most likely represent an attempt to imitate ancient coins that were somewhat familiar to the users, but with calculated alterations that would set them apart from the emulated coins.

Many of these coins flowed into Britain because of close social and economic relations with Gaul, and they seem to have served the needs of both regions equally well. When Caesar invaded Britain in 55 B.C., it was because of the strong ties between the Belgic tribes of north Gaul and the Belgic conquerors of southern Britain. These early imported coins later became influential models for the first coins made in Britain, and many of them are very similar in appearance.

Other interesting examples of early coins of this genre include low-grade silver (billon) produced for northwest Gaul and the Channel Islands, and cast copper/tin (potin) pieces made for use as token coinage. Designs on these coins are abstract in the extreme, but with imagination they can be identified as representing a head on one side and a horse on the other.

Channel Islands billon stater, circa 75–50 B.C. (top); Celtic potin unit, first century B.C. (bottom). (1.4x actual size)

Gallo-Belgic gold staters are usually found in Very Fine or better condition, and priced at around $700. The attractive Channel Islands coins are often seen in wretched condition, but a nice specimen can occasionally be found for $150. The potin, or tin, coins are difficult to locate in any decent condition. Respectable specimens are usually priced at $150 to $200.

3.33x actual size

Britannia Waives the Rules

ROMAN BRITAIN. GETA. SESTERTIUS. 209–211

The Roman occupation of Britain progressed under leadership of several emperors who followed Julius Caesar. Claudius was the first to issue coins that contained any reference to the occupation, but those were made more for propaganda purposes than as a convenient currency for the islands. In time, numerous lightweight local imitations of Claudius's bronze coins made their appearance and served commercial needs.

Among the more famous Roman rulers of this time is Hadrian, the emperor who ruled from A.D. 96 to 138. Although he did not issue coins specifically for use in Britain, many of his issues did circulate there, and he stayed there for a time during visits through his vast empire. He is best known as the builder of an elaborate frontier system in northern England known as Hadrian's Wall, much of which is still standing today.

The most popular coins of Roman Britain are those made by Emperor Septimius Severus and his sons Caracalla and Geta. The typical example shown here was made by Geta shortly after he went to Britain in 208. While there, he spent much of his time in and around London and York, and was elevated to the rank of Augustus by his father in 209. He served jointly with his father and brother until his death in 211. Coins of all three of these Roman emperors proclaim their victory over the Britons through use of titles and figural representations. Notable among the many "Britannia" coin types are those that show a seated figure of Victory holding a shield, and the legend VICTORIAE BRITTANNICAE or some variation. Other types show standing Victories, or a single figure seated, holding a shield and spear. On some, only the simple legend BRITANNIA is shown. On the obverse of all these coins, the emperors are named "Augustus Britannia," or some variation thereof. The legend VICT BRIT used on many of these coins refers to Roman success in military campaigns in northern Britain beyond the provincial frontier.

The Victory or captivity designs proclaimed the Roman rule of the islands, but for some strange reason, in time the figure of Britannia came to be seen as a representation of Britain and was used as a patriotic design on the copper coins of Charles II beginning in 1672. (This despite the persistent rumor that it was the king's mistress who posed for the seated figure.) Thereafter it became a nationalistic symbol on numerous English coins, and by an even stranger twist of fate the same seated figure morphed into Liberty on some colonial coins of early America. Then in 1836, she blossomed into the Liberty Seated design on many United States coins minted up until 1891.

Titles and figures on the coins of the Roman emperors proclaimed their victory over the Britons.

Coins of Roman Britain are always popular with collectors of both Roman and British monies. Those with Britannia designs are particularly desirable and command premium prices. The much-admired Seated Britannia sestertius of Geta is valued from **$500** in Fine condition to **$1,500** in Very Fine.

2x actual size

Ready or Not

Anglo-Saxon Britain. Aethelred II. Silver Penny. 978–1016

Aethelred II is better known as Aethelred the Unready. He earned the appellation not from being unprepared for anything in particular, but because he was rather inept in many ways. An unfounded myth holds that he was not ready for the coming of the millennium, which many believed would mark the end of the world. Concerns at that time were much worse than the fears that gripped many at the beginning of the third millennium, but were equally without foundation.

Aethelred the Unready tried to secure peace by paying the Danes a ransom of 10,000 pounds of silver.

Athelred's reign began at a time when England was enjoying relative prosperity. His lack of leadership and reliance on the friends he appointed to high positions soon put the country in jeopardy from a constant threat of invasion by the Danes. Fear became reality in 980 when the Danes descended in force. Faced with an untenable position, and with little will to fight, Aethelred attempted to secure a peace in 991 by agreeing to pay a ransom of 10,000 pounds of silver in what has become known as *danegeld*.

Three years later another payment was demanded. That time it was 16,000 pounds of silver, and in 1002 yet another payment—of 24,000 pounds—was required. This drain on the nation was unbearable, and England quickly sank into a state of decline that undid all of the progress that had been made since the time of the Romans. It was a time of corruption, favoritism, and plotting that held little hope for a positive resolution. England was virtually bankrupt and starving.

As the decay continued Aethelred became more neurotic, and in fear of further attacks he ordered all resident Danes to be killed. He selected November 13, 1002, as the day of infamy. Among the thousands who were killed was the sister of the king of Denmark. The dreadful act incited further hostilities and a demand for even more danegeld. Aethelred then agreed to a payment of 36,000 pounds of silver in a final attempt to buy peace.

By 1014 Aethelred had lost his control of England and fled to Normandy for protection. Cnut, the son of King Swegn of Denmark, then seized power and agreed to a division of the country with Eadmund Ironsides, the son of Aethelred. Upon Aethelred's death in 1016, Cnut secured the control of all England, and later married Emma of Normandy, the widow of Aethelred.

The saga of Aethelred the Unready is one of those scarcely remembered chronicles that is hardly explained by the name "unready" that he earned. The appellation was derived from the Anglo-Saxon word *unread*, meaning "without counsel."

Several types of silver pennies were made by Aethelred II during his short reign. The more common types range in value from **$250** in Fine condition to **$450** or more for one that is Very Fine. Rare types command prices in excess of **$2,000**.

3x actual size

Patron Saint of Kings

Anglo-Saxon. Edward the Confessor. Silver Penny. 1042–1066

Edward (called "the Confessor") was the son of Aethelred II and Emma of Normandy. His reign was quite different from that of his father, and was marked by peace and prosperity. While still a youngster, he and his brother Alfred were taken to Normandy in 1013 by their mother (the sister of Normandy's duke Richard II), to escape the Danish occupation of England. During this period of exile, Edward was greatly influenced by Norman customs, and developed a keen sense of personal piety and resolve.

In 1036 Edward returned to England with his brother Alfred in an attempt to remove his stepbrother Harold from power in what had become a part of the Danish empire. The abortive attempt resulted in Alfred's capture and death, and Edward was forced to return to Normandy to await a more favorable opportunity. That came in 1041 when he was invited back to England, and he ascended to the throne the following year.

Edward's rule in England was made difficult by three earls who held control of Wessex, Mercia, and Northumbria. His preference for Norman ways caused friction from Saxons and Danish nobles alike, and fostered a growing resentment by those who favored the old regime. Despite these adversities Edward accomplished many things to transform the English monarchy into its present form. He designed the royal seal and coronation customs, and was instrumental in the advancement of fresh art styles.

Edward's marriage in 1045 left no heir to the throne, and was termed "spiritual," after Edward refused to consummate it rather than break his vow of chastity. Upon his death in 1066, the most worthy claimant was his brother-in-law Harold, the son of Godwin, earl of Wessex. He defeated Harold of Norway who invaded the north, but was himself defeated and killed at the Battle of Hastings by William of Normandy, who conquered and unified all of England.

Edward's title, the Confessor, signifies that he has been canonized a saint of the church. He was a holy man, who reportedly performed several miracles, including the healing of people by touching them. At the time, there were two types of saints: martyrs, who were killed for their faith; and confessors, who died a natural death. In the Roman Catholic Church, Edward the Confessor is considered the patron saint of kings and difficult marriages. From 1190 to 1348, Edward was considered the patron saint of all England, until being replaced by Saint George.

Edward designed the English royal seal and coronation customs, and promoted fresh new styles of art.

Most of the types of silver pennies of Edward are relatively common for coins of that era. They are usually obtainable in Very Fine to Extra Fine condition at prices from $250 to $400. The portraits on many of these pieces are delightfully crude and charming.

3.16x actual size

The Norman Kings

England. William the Conqueror. Silver Penny. 1066–1087

William the Conqueror is another colorful name held firm in the minds of everyone interested in the history of England. His role at the Battle of Hastings and the date 1066 are familiar to most coin collectors as well, especially those who enjoy medieval hammered coins.

William I, also known as William of Normandy, William the Bastard, and William the Conqueror, was the illegitimate son of Duke Robert the Devil and a tanner's daughter. He based his claim to the throne on a promise made to him by King Edward the Confessor, who was his second cousin. Upon Edward's death in 1066, a council of barons elected Edward's brother-in-law, Harold Godwinson, instead of William. This so angered William that he initiated an invasion from Normandy, and in the ensuing battle Harold was killed and his army defeated.

The obverse of William's coins contains a sketchy portrait of this bold king of all England.

The coins of William the Conqueror are similar to those of his Anglo-Saxon predecessors and consist entirely of silver pennies that were made at satellite mints throughout the kingdom. Eight types were made, but the only relatively common pieces are those made late in his reign with the inscription PAXS (Peace) on the reverse. The obverse of his coins contains a sketchy portrait of this bold king of all England. Many high-grade examples were found in a hoard discovered early in the 19th century and have supplied collectors with examples that otherwise would have been very costly. This fortunate discovery made coins of this king very popular and desirable. The consistent high quality of William's coins was achieved by making most of the dies in London and carefully controlling the minters.

During William's long reign, he completed a survey record of all England in 1086, known as the Doomsday Book. One of the main purposes of the survey was to determine the extent of his new kingdom. It also identified landowners so that they could be taxed according to their assets. Records written in the Doomsday Book were considered final and binding with no appeal, and it was given the name *Doomsday* to emphasize the notion of being the Last Judgment.

The Norman invasion of England by William I on October 14, 1066, defeated the Anglo-Saxon army and all other claimants to the throne. It was the last time England has ever been conquered by a foreign power.

Silver pennies of William the Conqueror are very popular and always in high demand by collectors. The PAXS type coins are the most readily available and the least costly. They are also desirable because they are usually obtainable in Extremely Fine or better condition at prices beginning around $700. Pieces that have weak letters or an indistinct portrait are worth somewhat less.

3x actual size

Come to My Party

ENGLAND. HENRY I. SILVER PENNY. 1100–1135

The fourth son of William the Conqueror succeeded his older brother, William II Rufus, as heir to the English throne in 1100, after Rufus was killed in a hunting accident. Henry I was called "Beauclerc" because of his scholarly interests; he was also termed the "Lion of Justice" for the many improvements he made in the administrative and legislative practices of that time. However, there was also a dark side to his personality.

Henry's ascension to the throne was somewhat clouded with misgiving about the way his brother Rufus died so conveniently while his other older brother Robert Curthose was away on the Crusades. Henry later captured and imprisoned Robert, and after Robert tried to escape, Henry had his eyes burnt out to prevent any further attempt. His reign is also noted for its political opportunism, the integration of the divided Anglo-Saxons and Normans within his kingdom, and his controversial decision to name his daughter as his heir.

Throughout his reign, Henry was known for many brutal acts. He once threw a man from the tower of Rouen, and often had his enemies blinded, including several members of his own family. In a famous numismatic incident called the "Assize of the Moneyers," Henry invited all of the minters in England to a Christmas party in 1124 and proceeded to have those who were suspected of issuing lightweight coins mutilated by cutting off their hands and other unmentionable parts.

Also around this time an attempt was made to reconcile difficulties in Normandy through the marriage of his eldest son William to the daughter of the count of Anjou. A further union was made when Henry's daughter Matilda married the count's son, Geoffrey Plantagenet. In his expansion of power, Henry was in need of financial support, which he sought through increased activities of centralized government. As another way to increase tax revenues, he also granted a charter to the Jews that allowed them to settle in England.

Henry died in 1135 from overindulgence and food poisoning. The barons who had sworn allegiance to his daughter reneged on their resolve, and instead encouraged Henry's nephew, Stephen of Blois, to claim the throne with their support. This resulted in a vicious civil war that pitted Matilda against the barons and Stephen. Stephen naming Matilda's son (Henry II) as his heir in 1153 eventually settled the dispute.

More than a dozen different designs were used for Henry's silver pennies. He also issued a rare silver halfpenny. All of his coins are scarce and desirable. Many of these coins show signs of small cuts and marks that were done officially to show that the pieces are made of good silver. Very Fine condition pieces are priced at or above $500. A nice Fine coin might still be purchased at $300 or less, but all of his issues are scarce and difficult to locate.

Henry was called "Beauclerc" because of his scholarly interests; however, there was also a dark side to his personality. . . .

3.33x actual size

I'm Henry the Eighth, I Am

England. Henry VIII. Silver Groat. 1509–1547

It is unfortunate that a man so closely linked to English history should be mostly remembered for his six wives. That is the case with Henry VIII, son of Henry VII, who ascended to the throne upon his father's death in 1509. He began his connubial escapades early in life when he was contracted to marry his brother's widow, Catherine of Aragon. It was a union that ended in divorce, and helped plant the seed of the Protestant Reformation. The pope refused to accept Henry's right to separate, so Henry broke ties with Rome.

Parliament supported Henry's decision and approved of his assuming the title of Protector and Supreme Head of the Church of England. With this authority he did away with monasteries to further enhance his position and to strip them of their wealth. After gaining control of the Church, he canceled their minting privileges; from that point forward, all mints were controlled by the king.

Ireland silver groat (1534–1540) of Henry VIII. (1.25x actual size)

Henry's early coinage began with issues that were similar to those of his father, but in 1526 the value of all gold coins was increased by about 10%, in response to the rising price of bullion and to prevent coins from being exported. Other changes followed, and toward the end of his reign coinage had become so debased that everyone hated it. His finances were in such a shambles due to his extravagances that they could only be bolstered by issuing "silver" coins with two-thirds copper. The debased issues were so disliked that they earned him the name "Old Copper Nose," in reference to their appearance when the silver coating wore away, leaving his portrait showing signs of the deceit underneath.

The fate of Henry's wives varied. Anne Boleyn, his second (and mother of Elizabeth I), was beheaded. She was followed by Jane Seymour, who died; Anne of Cleves received a divorce. Catherine Howard, his fifth wife, was beheaded, and Catherine Parr managed to outlive the king. Henry's only son, Edward VI, assumed the throne upon the king's death in 1547; however, he was too young to rule so the duke of Somerset, his uncle, ruled the country and established it as a Protestant state. Eventually the throne went to Henry's daughter Elizabeth, who is another of the popular monarchs high on the want-list of many coin collectors.

Among the many issues of Henry VIII, silver groats are some of the most popular because they are affordable, and they graphically show the debasement of his coinage. Early pieces are attractive, well made, and of fine silver. Later issues are poorly made and often show the base-metal interior. Collectors have many choices of denominations and metals. Gold is scarce, but fine, large silver pieces are usually available. A Very Fine groat (fourpence) will be priced at about $300.

2.5x actual size

Shakespeare's England

England. Elizabeth I. Silver Sixpence. 1561

"Come on, there is sixpence for you—let's have a song."
Twelfth Night, II. iii. 32.

William Shakespeare was born in 1564 during the reign of Queen Elizabeth I, and he died in 1616 while King James was in power. In his many plays he often used coins and coin terms to create puns and familiar scenes. His knowledge of contemporary coins, and those of other times and cultures, was remarkable. Although not always historically accurate about every coin brought into his plays, Shakespeare had a flair for conveying his intended meaning through coins in a way that would have been understandable to his audiences.

Coins were an extremely important part of daily life in the 16th century. They were objects of value and contained a full measure of gold or silver. Unlike the abstract paper and electronic money of today, precious-metal coins were a tangible commodity familiar to all in everyday experiences.

The age of Queen Elizabeth I was also a time of change and innovation for English coinage. New denominations and fresh designs were introduced, while the shoddy debased coins of her father Henry VIII were driven out of circulation. One of the most remarkable modernizations was an attempt to use a screw press for the production of coins. Previously, all coins had been made by hand-hammering each blank of metal. The screw press provided greater force, and produced uniformly struck pieces that were neat, attractive, and nearly round. Unfortunately, the French minter who was contracted to use the newly invented screw press was shunned by traditional mint workers, and soon he was forced to leave the Tower Mint. However, Eloye Mestrell—who produced the beautiful milled coins for the queen from 1561 to 1575—was not to be denied. While unemployed, he turned his talent to making his own dies and imitation coins, until he was caught and hanged in 1577 as a counterfeiter.

Shakespeare had a flair for conveying his intended meanings through references to coins.

Another unique innovation in the coinage of Elizabeth I was the use of a rose placed at the back of her head on silver coins of every alternate denomination (specifically, the rose was placed on the threepence, not on the fourpence, on the sixpence, not on the twelvepence, etc.). This simple designation made it easy for everyone to distinguish coins of similar size that did not contain any other indication of value. Elizabeth was also first to use a long sequence of Christian dates on some of her silver coins; she also had a secret indication (a "privy mark") on her coinage to tell exactly when the coins were made.

The rose behind the bust on these coins gave chance for Shakespeare to add one of his charming numismatic puns in *King John*, I. i. 143. Here he brings into play the fact that the three-farthings coin is so small that the bust of Elizabeth is cramped. He

2.40x actual size

alludes to that in the following line: "My face so thin, that in mine ear I durst not stick a rose, lest men should say, 'Look, where three-farthings goes!'"

Elizabeth was one of England's most popular monarchs, and the country prospered under her direction. It was at this time that the Renaissance was beginning throughout Europe, and business and trade developed rapidly. The queen worked hard to keep her country at peace because she detested war. Even so, in 1588 the tension between Spain and England had grown to the point of open combat. Spain wanted to expand control of the Atlantic trade routes, and hoped that England could be made to return to the Catholic faith. King Philip II of Spain (husband to England's Queen Mary, 1554 to 1558) had an armada of 130 warships and was preparing to attack England. Elizabeth, however, rallied her troops to action with a stirring speech that won the day.

Elizabeth rallied her troops to action with a stirring speech that won the day.

With the defeat of the Spanish armada, England was firmly established as a world power. Silver captured from Spanish ships was used to make the impressive array of fine silver coins that mark Elizabeth's reign. The queen was the first to accommodate trade by making not only large-size coins, but also a number of smaller pieces that were more suitable to everyday commerce. Her greatest numismatic triumph came in 1560 with new issues that restored the old fineness and drove out debased and foreign money.

Elizabeth's portrait became cramped on some of her small-denomination coins. (Actual size)

Sixpence of Elizabeth are in demand for their historical importance, their attractive design, and their long run of dates that extends from 1561 to 1602. They are distinguished by collectors as either hammered or milled, and examples of both styles are often added to their sets. Pieces in Fine condition are acceptable, but will often have letters or part of the design weakly struck. They are usually available for less than $125. Very Fine coins sell at $300 to $400, depending on how well struck they are. Milled pieces are usually much nicer in appearance and are worth about $100 more than their counterparts.

King of Scotland and England

England. James I. Silver Penny. 1619–1625

King James I of England was also recognized as James VI of Scotland. The dual title went to him in 1603 upon the death of Queen Elizabeth. When he ascended to the English throne, he had already been king of Scotland for 36 years. Like Elizabeth, he was a patron of the theater, and an admirer of playwright William Shakespeare. The two had a very special bond in their love of literature, and Shakespeare wrote his play *Macbeth* specifically for the king.

James VI was the son of Mary Queen of Scots, the cousin of Queen Elizabeth. The two were bitter enemies, and in 1567 Mary was forced to abdicate in favor of her year-old son. She was thereafter imprisoned in the Tower of London for many years and executed in 1587 for her part in the planned assassination of Queen Elizabeth. James never knew either of his parents, and the early years of his reign were under the guidance of tutors. He was a diligent student, and proficient in several languages and many disciplines.

Despite his frail health, James was intellectual and a very caring monarch who believed in the divine right of kings, and his duty to reign according to God's law and the public good. He was devoutly religious, and wrote extensively on many subjects. Among his many accomplishments, the greatest was his direction of an English translation of the Bible in 1611, which is now known as the King James Version. This effort, however, was widely criticized at the time by those he called papists, and created an ever-widening gap between Protestants and Catholics.

James ruled both England and Scotland wisely from 1603 to 1625. His coinage followed the tradition set by Elizabeth, and consisted of a wide range of denominations made of fine gold and silver. He also added a convenient copper farthing at the request of his subjects. These coins were made under private contract with Lord Harington in 1613 and the duke of Lennox in later years.

James I was the first to call the empire Great Britain, to reflect his sovereignty over both England and Scotland, but friction between the two remained strong. His popularity also suffered from his reliance on court favorites, a weak foreign policy, and constant bickering with the Catholics. In 1605 Guy Fawkes attempted to blow up Parliament when the king was scheduled to be there. The failed effort is still remembered each year in England on November 5, and is known as Guy Fawkes Night.

The coin selected here to represent this period in history is a silver penny. It is significant because the term *penny* was used in the King James Bible as an alternate word for the Roman silver coin more precisely known as a denarius. A silver penny of James is very similar in diameter to the old Roman coins, and a term that would have been easier to understand in the 17th century. An Extremely Fine example of this coin is valued at $150.

The King James Bible referred to the Roman denarius as a penny, *which would have been familiar to 17th-century readers.*

4.29x actual size

Turmoil and Disaster

England. Charles II. Silver Crown. 1666

There was little peace and tranquility during the reign of King Charles II of England, who ruled from 1660 to 1685. He left much of the administration of the kingdom to his ministers and pursued a lifestyle that was immoral and expensive. His early years were spent in exile in France, and he did not return to England until after the fall of Oliver Cromwell and the Commonwealth in 1660, at which time he ascended to the throne.

The products of new machines and talented engravers, Charles's coins were far superior to any of the past.

The kingdom was racked during this time by the great London plague of 1665 that took 75,000 lives and caused widespread hardships and strife. Known as the bubonic plague, or Black Death, the pandemic was likely halted only by more tragedy in the form of the great fire of London in 1666. Most of the city was destroyed in the fire, and not rebuilt until many years later, primarily under the direction of master architect Christopher Wren.

Added to the turmoil of this troubled king's reign was an outbreak of hostilities with the Dutch that resulted in yet another Anglo-Dutch War that lasted from 1664 to 1667. The conflict ended with negotiations called the Peace of Breda, in which the Dutch relinquished control of parts of the North American continent, including New Netherlands (the present New York), in exchange for sugar factories on Surinam.

The numismatic highlight of this reign was the introduction of machine-made coins. Talented engravers were appointed to design the king's coins, and new minting equipment resulted in coins that are far superior to anything in the past. It now became possible to make dollar-size "crowns" to compete with other European currency, and to have a modern-looking coinage equal to that of any other country. At this time, dates were consistently added to these coins, and the edges were marked with lettering to prevent clipping or shaving away bits of the metal.

The minting of halfpenny and farthing coins in copper and tin was also introduced to facilitate small transactions. The design on these coins was a resurrection of the old Seated Britannia design taken from Roman coins. The pieces made of tin did not hold up well and were soon replaced by the copper coins. The few tin pieces that have survived until today are scarce and valuable relics of this era. This monarch also initiated the custom of issuing specially made silver one pence, twopence, threepence, and fourpence coins for use as gifts in the traditional Maundy Ceremony on the king's birthday.

Many of the coins of Charles II are relatively common. They are usually well made and available in high grade at modest prices. A favorite example for this reign is the crown coin of 1666 that was made at the height of turmoil and tribulation brought on by the war, the plague, and the great fire of London. Examples of these silver crowns are usually priced at about $150 for a Fine piece to $700 for Very Fine or better.

1.45x actual size

Queen Anne's Wars

England. George II. Silver Half Crown. 1746
England. Queen Anne. Silver Half Crown. 1703

The coins of Queen Anne, who ruled from 1702 to 1714, are of interest to collectors for several reasons. None are as adventuresome as the unusual pieces made in 1702 and 1703 bearing the word VIGO beneath her portrait. The reason for this unprecedented departure from the norm came in October 1702, following a successful Anglo-Dutch battle with the Spanish fleet.

Gold, silver, and valuable cargos had been held at Spanish-American ports for three years while Spain was engaged in the War of Succession. When a French escort fleet finally came to help, 17 vessels were loaded with treasure and set out for Cadiz (Spain). Meanwhile, the Spanish were engaging the British and Dutch fleets at Cadiz and another British fleet was at sea in their path. The convoy received news of the situation, and detoured for Vigo Bay in Galicia, Spain, to wait for things to quiet down.

The British fleet, soundly defeated in the battle at Cadiz, was limping home when the commander of the British ship *Pembroke* received news about the treasure fleet. The temptation of such a prize was beyond resistance. The British fleet made straight for Vigo Bay and engaged the Spanish in a battle that lasted for about two hours before the poorly protected treasure ships were defeated. In what was one of the costliest naval engagements 13 French and Spanish ships were taken and 2,000 men perished. The British and Dutch lost 800 men and another 500 were wounded. Millions of pieces of eight were captured, along with gold and other booty that was taken back to England to be made into coin of the realm.

The sparkling new coins that were made from these spoils of war were inscribed with the word VIGO for all the world to forever be reminded of this famous battle. So popular was this form of propaganda that it was repeated some 43 years later by King George II, when he added the word LIMA to some of his coins. (The silver for that issue, dated 1745 and 1746, was made from the treasure brought back to England by Admiral Anson in 1744. These coins were minted to celebrate British harassment of the Spanish colonies in the New World.)

Queen Anne is also remembered for other bloody battles on both sides of the Atlantic. Perhaps most notable among her conquests were the raid on Deerfield, Massachusetts, in 1704 and the attempt to capture Quebec. Her quarrels with Scotland were bitter, but ended with the Act of Union in 1707, under which the two kingdoms were officially united as Great Britain. Anne died in 1714, and although she had 17 children, none of them survived to assume the throne.

Silver half crown of George II, 1746. (.88x actual size)

A silver shilling of Queen Anne in Extremely Fine condition will cost about $500. One in Fine will be under $100. Other denominations are priced about the same. Coins of George II with the LIMA inscription are equally interesting, and are priced similar to the VIGO pieces.

1.62x actual size

CAROL·IIII·D·G·HISP·ET IND·R·
·1799·

CHAPTER 7

The Reign in Spain

Voyage of Discovery

Spain. Ferdinand and Isabella. Gold Double Excelente. Circa 1492

Numerous myths and misconceptions surround the life and times of Christopher Columbus. Most people remember only that he received backing from the king and queen of Spain, and set out to look for gold and spices in the Indies, landing instead in America. They know the names of his three ships, and the date they made landfall. Fewer people are aware of the unpleasant aftermath of his discovery, such as the many hardships he inflicted on the natives that he sold into slavery back in Spain.

Gold excelente of Spain, circa 1492. (Actual size)

Anyone who has ever wondered what the king and queen of Spain looked like in 1492, or what kind of coins were given to Columbus to finance his voyage of discovery, can satisfy that curiosity by examining a coin of that time and place. Such pieces do still exist, and not all are impounded in museums. Owning one of these coins is part of the joy of collecting, and an entertaining way to learn more about history than just can be found in books. The impressive gold coins of Ferdinand and Isabella are of special importance because they contain life-portraits of the monarchs, and because they are quite likely the very sort of money given to Columbus to start him on his way.

Like other European coins of the 15th century, the money of Ferdinand and Isabella was hand-hammered, and crude by modern standards. Yet, they produced a full range of gold, silver, and copper coins that were well made, with attractive designs. The portraits of the Catholic Monarchs that are shown on their gold coins are well crafted, and probably lifelike. (Interestingly, the bust of Ferdinand as shown on his coins was employed as a model for the unknown likeness of Columbus that was used on the United States Columbian Exposition commemorative half dollars of 1892 and 1893.) The silver and copper coins of this reign have ornate designs, but do not have the rulers' portraits. Gold 1- and 2-excelente coins, and extremely rare higher denominations, all show facing busts of the rulers. They are always eagerly sought by collectors.

The excelentes endured as the coin of the realm beyond the death of Isabella in 1504 and the demise of Ferdinand in 1516. Their grandson, Charles I, continued to mint similar coins until 1536. Dates were never shown on these coins, and it is impossible to tell which may have been used by the explorer, and which may have been made from gold brought back from the New World. Undoubtedly some must have been onboard during his third (1498) and fourth (1502) voyages. Legend holds that he used such coins to ask where similar metal could be found, and to show the natives the likeness of the king and queen.

A Very Fine gold excelente of Ferdinand and Isabella minted in Seville is priced today at about $700. Extremely Fine pieces are worth closer to $1,000. The double excelente is the most attractive and the most popular coin of this series. Extremely Fine specimens sell for $2,500 and are usually available with a little searching.

2.07x actual size

Money of the New World

Spain. Santo Domingo. Copper 4 Maravedís. Circa 1540

The concept of coins as money came late to the Americas. There was little need for coins as a store of value in the agrarian societies where commerce was based largely on trade, barter, and allegiance to the ruler. With the Spanish infusion, natives soon learned that their gold and silver ornaments were of more than passing interest to the foreigners, and that tobacco, spices, and other commodities were highly valued exports.

Ornaments of gold, silver, and copper, trade beads, tools, and weapons were popular everywhere in both North and South America. Over time, a few specialized items became more in demand, and were accepted by several cultures as standard bartering items. Aztecs in New Spain (Mexico) used strange copper "hide scrapers" in their transactions. These unusual items apparently served no functional purpose except for use in trade. They are much too thin to be used as tools, but the bright shiny copper apparently made them highly coveted as adornments. Originally called *hacha de cobre*, or "copper hatchets," and now called *coas*, they were valued in cacao beans, themselves a valuable commodity.

The Incas of Peru normally worked for the good of the state in a welfare society, while the nobility lived in a luxury that afforded them gold and silver ornaments and utensils. Their numerous small gold objects may very well have served as trade items, but there is scant documentation to confirm this. What is clear is that the conquistadors took as much of their precious metal as possible and carried it home to Spain. Stories of how the natives were abused and the land sacked need not be repeated here, except to add that little of the national treasures of precious metal items survived the onslaught, and very few of their golden trade items are known outside of museums.

The first actual coins used in New Spain were copper 2- and 4-maravedís pieces intended to circulate in Santo Domingo. They were made in Seville and sent there for use as small change, but the natives rejected them and preferred to use traditional barter items. Around 1542, similar coins were made at the Mexico City mint, but the natives also refused to accept them. Despite the viceroy's orders and threat of severe punishment, nothing could prevent the Indians from throwing them into the gutters or into Lake Texcoco "that they might never more be seen." Many of the pieces that are in collections today have been recovered from the lake during drainage operations, and show signs of corrosion from their long immersion.

Copper maravedís of Mexico. (Actual size)

In 1550, the Mexico City mint stopped coining copper pieces because of the misuse by the Indians, and it was officially outlawed by royal decree in 1565. A copper coinage was not attempted again in New Spain until 1814.

2.40x actual size

Two- and 4-maravedís coins of Santo Domingo sell for $100 or less in Very Fine. The early copper coins made in Mexico are rarely available in any grade above Fine, and sell for $400 and up. Copper "hatchet money" will cost around $75. While Inca gold is virtually unavailable, cacao beans are often sold as novelties for 25¢ each.

Copper hacha de cobre of Mexico. (reduced)

Gold tumi (ceremonial knife) of Incan Peru. (Actual size)

Spanish-American Cobs

Mexico. Philip III. Silver 8 Reales. 1598—1605

The oddly shaped coins of Spanish America known as cobs are not fully appreciated by collectors, who sometimes think of them as being ugly, difficult to decipher, and poorly made. In reality, they are the results of a primitive production that served the purpose of transporting silver from the New World back to Spain, and on its way to international trade. Their place in lore and history, their rustic charm, and their appeal to treasure hunters far overshadow their crudeness. These are "manly" coins of the buccaneers of old that deserve a spot in every coin cabinet.

The word *cob* may have been derived from an old English word for a lump or piece of coal, but a more plausible explanation is that it comes from the phrase *cabo de barra*, meaning the end of a bar. In Spanish, these coins are more properly known as *macuquina*. Their crudeness comes from the inexperience of minters at the Mexico mint that first began operations in 1535. Blanks for these coins were cut from a ribbon of metal, with little regard for shape or thickness. Coins were then hammered with hand-held dies in a mass-production endeavor that sometimes left the pieces barely recognizable, although of full weight and proper value.

Cobs were made extensively from 1580 to 1732 at several mints in Spain and in the New World. The earliest pieces were not dated. Beginning around 1605 dates were added, but are rarely legible; in some cases as many as three dates were used on the coins in hopes that one might be readable. In the New World, cobs were made from local silver in Peru, Mexico City, Bolivia, Colombia, and Guatemala. Each of the Spanish-American mints used a slightly different design so their work could be recognized.

Cob coinage was struck in many denominations, from the tiny medio, or half real, to the dollar-size 8 reales or "piece of eight," which contained nearly one ounce of silver. Coins of 1, 2, and 4 reales were produced in quantities, but none as vast as the ubiquitous pieces of eight. Their use in international trade is legendary, as they were welcomed and used around the world. They were also a prime target of pirate ships everywhere.

No tale of sunken treasure is ever complete without pieces of eight. Yes, the stories are largely true, and an untold fortune in these coins still lies at the bottom of the sea where ships were lost to storms on their way back to Spain laden with gold and silver from the Americas. Throughout the years some of these unfortunate ships have been recovered—a welcome source for collectors seeking examples of cob coins. Unfortunately many of those that have rested in the ocean for nearly 400 years are now corroded and uglier than ever. Still, little can diminish the mystique of old cobs, or their appeal to collectors.

The value of cobs varies with many factors. Issuer, date, and mint are of first importance. Condition has a bearing on price, as does the number of dates that are legible. Any attractive cob should be worth $100 and up. Rare pieces may be worth several thousand dollars.

No tale of sunken treasure is complete without pieces of eight. And yes, the stories are largely true. . .

1.62x actual size

An International Scandal

Bolivia. Philip IIII. Silver 8 Reales. 1652

When the quality and fineness of Potosí coins declined, officials from Madrid sentenced the minters to death.

The Lima mint was closed temporarily in 1588, leaving Potosí as the only operating mint in the viceroyalty of Peru for nearly a century. In that time the mint continued to produce cob coinage, but it became obvious that the appearance and even the precious-metal fineness of these coins was not up to Spanish standards. In terms of workmanship 1617 marked a low point, bringing a concerned inquiry from the king. Reforms in the appearance of the coins were made but the problems were not eliminated, and the Lima coinage eventually became even more debased and devaluated. A new investigation by Madrid officials resulted in death sentences for those responsible and a general recall of the deficient 4- and 8-reales coins.

In 1652 a new coinage was ordered for Potosí in an effort to eradicate the embarrassment of the faulty coins of the past. The revised design contained the Spanish lions and castles divided by the cross of Jerusalem. Below the cross was the date, and the king's name was in the legend. To the left of the cross was the letter P, and to the right the assayer's initial. The obverse was divided into nine compartments by two upright pillars and two horizontal bands. Under the pillars: stylized waves, with the date in four figures in the legend. The motto PLUS ULTRA ("More Beyond") filled the middle horizontal range of compartments.

In the center of the upper range was the denomination, and in the middle of the bottom range was the date, abbreviated to only the last two figures. The assayer's initial was also added to the design on this side. The assayer was identified on both sides of each coin in several different places, with the date shown in three spots. The same basic design was used on all denominations from 1 real to 8 reales. This combination, along with a much more experienced and careful minting operation, restored worldwide confidence in Lima's coinage. The new designs that were first struck in 1652 were not without experimental quirks, and at least seven different varieties were made before the final design was settled. (The piece shown here somehow failed to indicate the denomination.)

An acute shortage of coins resulted from the melting of the older debased coinage, and in 1658 the Lima mint was unofficially reopened after a 71-year hiatus. The revised "pillars and waves" design was used on those coins, but with a slightly different arrangement of the waves to distinguish them. By 1682, Lima had grown increasingly wealthy from the bustling trade with Spanish fleets, and a wall was built around the city to discourage thieves and pirates.

Finely made cob coins of Potosí, dated after 1651, are some of the more attractive coins of this era, and are in high demand by collectors. Those with the significant date of 1652 are particularly well appreciated. Specimens in Very Fine condition, with two or three dates showing, trade at prices around $600 or more. Later dates or those without any date showing are often available for $100.

1.58x actual size

Pieces of Eight

Mexico. Charles III. Silver 8 Reales. 1760

Everyone who has ever read tales of pirates, plunder, and intrigue is familiar with the legendary gold doubloons and pieces of eight. These coins were used throughout the world in international trade and as a store of wealth in coin and bullion form. The Spanish doubloon was a large gold coin that contained nearly a full ounce of gold, and the 8-reales coin, or piece of eight, was its counterpart that contained nearly one ounce of silver. These were the coins authorized by the Spanish kings for use in their American possessions, for international trade, and as a convenient means of transporting precious metals from their mines in the New World.

Millions of dollars' worth of these coins were transported back and forth across the Atlantic, enriching the Spanish royal coffers. The pieces of eight in particular were well known throughout the world, and were especially popular in British colonial America, where they were known as Pillar dollars. When the first United States coins were contemplated in 1786, the founding fathers decided to use the exact size and weight of the Spanish-American dollar as a basis for their new coinage system. Many collectors of United States coinage consider the Pillar dollar to be the grandfather of all American coins, and strive to include at least one specimen in their sets.

The 8-reales coins, and their fractions of one half, one quarter, and one eighth, were used extensively throughout colonial America at a time when other European coins were in short supply. They even served as legal tender in this country until 1857, and became so much a part of the American economy that terms associated with them continue to be used up to the present. The most common expression referred to the U.S. quarter dollar as "two bits" because the fractional eighths of the piece of eight were originally called "bits." Similarly, stock-market quotes continued to price commodities in eighths of a dollar up until very recent times.

These coins were also responsible for the quarter-dollar denomination being chosen over a 20-cent piece, which is a true decimal division. The Spanish-American 2-reales coin (one quarter of the piece of eight) was so popular and convenient that the United States government adopted its size and denomination to make their first coins familiar, traditional, and easy to compute.

Pillar dollars, or "Two World" dollars, as they are often called, got their name from the two globes that are shown between the Pillars of Hercules, symbolizing Spain's rule over the old and new continents. The king's name and coat of arms grace the reverse of all of these pieces, which were minted from 1732 to 1771.

Many collectors of United States coinage consider the Pillar dollar to be the grandfather of all American coins.

Common-date Pillar dollars are usually priced in Very Fine condition at $175. Extremely Fine pieces are frequently available at $250, and Uncirculated coins are occasionally offered at about $600.

1.54x actual size

Gold Doubloons

PERU. PHILIP V. GOLD DOUBLOON. 1735

The *doubloon* is not an actual denomination, but is a popular term for the Spanish 8-escudo gold coin. The word comes from the large gold piece minted by the Catholic Monarchs Ferdinand and Isabella, who ruled from 1475 to 1504. It was known as the double excelente or *doble* ("two"). Somehow, over the years, the term was changed to *doubloon* and applied to the large gold pieces minted in Spain and the New World during the 17th and 18th centuries.

Both cob and milled doubloons were made. They look very much like the silver coins of that period, and the gold cob pieces are just as crude as the silver coins. The so-called milled pieces that were made by a screw press are, of course, much finer in appearance and look more like modern coins. Eight-escudo coins were produced in Spain and at New World mints in Lima, Mexico, Potosí, and Chile.

1799 gold doubloon of Charles IIII, Chile. (.81x actual size)

Legends about still-hidden pirate treasure containing chests of gold doubloons might well be true: countless numbers of these valuable coins were taken by pirates or lost at sea in the course of being transported across the ocean. Each doubloon was worth nearly a month's sustenance at that time, and thus was a precious amount of money. It is no wonder that these coins were the target of thievery and plunder. And no wonder treasure hunters today still search for hidden hoards and sunken treasures. Such things do still exist, and the thrill of finding those riches is captivating.

For collectors, owning a Spanish gold doubloon is nearly as gratifying as discovering one. It may also be less costly to buy a nice specimen than to spend a lifetime searching for one. Finding a lost treasure is an unlikely event, and those occasional coins that are washed ashore each year are usually worn or damaged from their long rest in the ocean. Amazingly, the current cost of common 18th-century doubloons is often less than double their gold content, or about the same as a common U.S. $20 gold coin. The reason that these coins are so inexpensive is that they were made in great quantities, and intended for use at the prevailing price of gold. They are a reminder of how the value of gold bullion keeps pace with inflation and the cost of living.

Lima- and Mexico-style cob doubloons are admired favorites among collectors because they are attractive and distinctive, but also because they served as money in this country for nearly 200 years. Their popularity and scarcity have made them somewhat more expensive than their later relatives, but a specimen of any type doubloon should be a welcome addition to every collection of worldwide or United States coins.

Cob doubloons from the mints of Lima and Mexico City can be obtained in grades ranging from Fine to Uncirculated. An average piece in Very Fine will cost about $2,500. Higher grades may be priced from $3,500 to $5,000. Milled doubloons, particularly the Bust type coins made at Spanish-American mints, are often available under $1,200 for Very Fine or better grades.

2.07x actual size

The Phantom Kings

Lima. Ferdinand VII. Imaginary Portrait 8 Reales. 1811

It is difficult to envision a time when a new king ascended to the throne and the public might not know what he looked like for several years. That is the way it was in an age before the modern conveniences of television, computers, and press reporting. Carrying news from Spain to the New World was a slow process in the 18th century, and the best way to spread the word of a new king was through images on his circulating coins.

When the old Pillar designs gave way to portrait coins in 1772, the reigning monarchs decreed that their names and images would grace each piece minted under their authority. To accomplish this, die-making tools were prepared in Spain and shipped to American mints. These implements, called "irons," consisted of metal matrixes containing the king's portrait, each of the necessary letters and numbers, various design elements, and the lion and castle parts of the shield. Steel rods were driven into the master matrixes to create the punches necessary for producing working dies. Under this system all of the coins minted from each of the American mints were uniform in appearance, varying only by their unique identifying mintmark.

The Spanish-American Bust coins, as they are known, were first issued by Charles III in 1772, and continued to be made by subsequent kings until the end of Spanish authority in 1825. Denominations made were 1/2 real, 1 real, 2 reales, 4 reales, and the large 8 reales (called "pieces of eight" or "Bust dollars"). These coins circulated freely all over the world and were widely respected for their faithful adherence to specified weight and fineness of the silver they contained. Several countries and colonies adopted them as their own currency and countermarked them with an identifying name or symbol in an effort to retain them as local money. Among those users were England, Canada, Brazil, many Spanish possessions in the West Indies, the early British American colonies, and even the independent United States until 1857. The dollars were equally popular in China, where many were "chopped" or punch-marked by merchants to verify their metal content.

Despite stringent quality controls imposed by Spain, there came times when the American minters were not supplied with new irons to make the necessary changes in the king's image or name. The time involved in shipping tools from Spain was too protracted to commence using new portraits in a timely manner. Consequently, in Lima after Charles III died in 1788 word did not reach the minters until many coins had been made with his name, portrait, and the date 1789. Then, with no indication of what the new king looked like, they began making coins with the name of Charles IV, but the same old bust of Charles III. It was not until 1791 that the new irons arrived and the bust and title were changed to that of Charles IV (Carolus IIII).

After Charles III died in 1788, word did not reach the minters in Lima until many coins had been made with his name, portrait, and the date 1789.

1.54x actual size

A similar series of events happened in Mexico during the transition from one king to another. There they used the bust and name of Charles III, and called him Charles IV in 1789 and 1790. In 1790 they also called him Charles IIII, and by 1792 they began using his real bust and preferred title of Charles IIII. The mints at Potosí, Nueva Guatemala, and Santiago, of course, all had similar problems, and made similar adjustments to accommodate the situation.

Potosí cob 8 reales of Philip V with counterstamp for use in Guatemala. (Actual size)

When King Charles IV abdicated in 1808 in favor of his son, Ferdinand VII, the American mints were again faced with the same circumstances, and had no knowledge of what the new king's portrait would look like. This time they took a different approach to the problem. Instead of using the old king's image, the mints at Mexico, Santiago, and Lima created their own version of an imaginary portrait and used that from 1808 to 1811 when the authorized irons arrived. The more timid minters in Potosí, Nueva Guatemala, and Bogotá continued to use the old king's portrait.

1801 Lima 8 reales of Charles IIII, with Brazil counterstamp. (Actual size)

A comprehensive collection of Spanish-American Bust dollars would consist of very many dates, mints, titles, kings, and styles of imagery. Few collectors accept the challenge, but at least one or more of these intriguing coins must be included in any collection for appreciation of this important chapter in the history of world coinage. Their role as the basis of the United States dollar coin is enough to qualify them as a key part of the nation's numismatic history.

Chopmarked dollars circulated extensively in China. (Actual size)

Spanish-American Bust dollars are not particularly scarce, and common dates or varieties are plentiful in all grades. Typical examples in Extremely Fine will cost about $150 or less. A coin in Fine or better with Chinese chopmarks may cost only about $25. Those counterstamped by merchants of other nations can be worth up to $500 or more.

Two Heads Not Worth a Crown

Charles III and George III. 8 Reales. 1794

In Britain from 1797 to 1804 there was a serious shortage of large silver coins because no crowns (dollar-size coins) had been issued since 1751, during the reign of George II. To remedy this situation quantities of captured Spanish 8-reales coins, and a few smaller denominations, were counterstamped to validate them for use in Britain. The large pieces were supposed to be accepted as "dollars" or crowns, but were officially valued at only 4 shillings, 9 pence each (instead of the normal 5 shillings for a crown). The plan was an expedient that worked, but the coins were unpopular and eventually most of them found their way back to the Royal Mint, where they were melted and their silver used to make new coins of the realm.

The captured Spanish coins used in this venture were mostly pieces of eight of Charles III, but other foreign coins were in the booty, including French ecus and a few United States dollars. The validation marks that were applied to the coins were small hallmark punches showing the head of Britain's King George III in an either oval or hexagonal frame. Neither King Charles nor George was particularly popular in either Spain or England, as both men were weak rulers. Charles abdicated in favor of his son Ferdinand in 1808 after he had lost the island of Hispaniola to the French in 1795 and ceded Louisiana to them in 1800. George was sickly during the waning years of his reign, and England was wracked by the War of Succession, which cost it its American colonies.

Using the captured Spanish dollars as emergency money was an economic necessity, but it was resented by nearly everyone. The coins soon became the butt of jokers who were quick to point out, "The two kings' heads are not worth a crown," as a reference to their value of only 4 shillings, 9 pence. Another popular quip stated, "The wise men of London, to make their coins pass, put the head of a fool on the neck of an ass."

Those who took advantage of the situation by privately marking counterfeit coins with a fake counterstamp (in order to more easily pass them to the unwary) further compromised the undertaking. By 1804 the experiment was seen as a total failure and many of the coins were taken back to the mint to be melted or overstamped with new dies and made into Bank of England dollars. These coins were made with attractive dies showing a large bust of the king on the obverse and seated Britannia on the reverse. The legend FIVE SHILLINGS BANK OF ENGLAND added to the credibility of the new issue and solved the dilemma.

Using captured Spanish dollars as emergency money was a resented necessity.

Counterstamped 8-reales coins of Charles III are not often found in condition higher than Extremely Fine. The usual grades range from Very Fine to Extremely Fine and are apt to be priced at about $500. Beware of counterfeit coins with either genuine or false countermarks, and counterfeit hallmarks on genuine coins. There are many such deceptive pieces, and they are, of course, worth much less than the genuine pieces.

1.45x actual size

The First Mexican Peso

MEXICO. EMPEROR MAXIMILIAN. SILVER PESO. 1866

Emperor Maximilian of Mexico was one of those unfortunate men of history who happened to be in the wrong place at the wrong time. Despite his good intentions, skill, and ability, his short reign was unappreciated and cut short by a number of ill-fated circumstances. One of his lasting legacies is numismatic: he is credited with introducing the peso denomination as a decimal coin to replace the old Spanish piece of eight. The change brought Mexican coinage into line with other decimal-oriented monetary units, and made the peso a much sought after coin in international trade.

Maximilian quickly realized he was but a pawn of the European powers.

Maximilian's mission to the New World began in 1864 when he reluctantly agreed to accept an appointment by Napoleon III of France to serve as emperor of Mexico. The unusual arrangement was as a result of Mexico's default on debts owed to several European nations, and the defunct governance of President Benito Juárez. In the following reorganization of power, Napoleon persuaded Maximilian, brother of Austrian emperor Franz Joseph, to "accept the crown of Mexico." It was a bold move that worked only because the United States was embroiled in a civil war of its own at that time and unable to uphold its Monroe Doctrine commitment to protect the Western Hemisphere from European encroachments.

From the very outset Maximilian found himself involved in serious difficulties because Mexican liberals led by Juárez refused to recognize his rule. There was continuous warfare between his French troops and the Mexican republicans. Maximilian's position was politically, economically, and strategically impossible to maintain, and he quickly realized he was but a pawn of European powers. He lost the support of conservatives and clerics who were angered by his support of many of the programs begun by Juárez.

Frustrated by the affairs of state, in time Maximilian became more interested in botany and butterfly collecting. His beloved wife Carlota, the daughter of Leopold I, king of Belgium, fought valiantly to maintain his support from France, but ultimately went out of her mind with grief and was institutionalized for the rest of her life.

The last of the French troops departed from Mexico in 1867. Emperor Maximilian was quickly captured and shot by a firing squad, after which Benito Juárez was restored as president of the Republic. While in power the emperor and empress had set up residence in Chapultepec Castle and ordered a wide avenue cut through the city from Chapultepec to the city center. Originally named Avenue of the Empress, it is today Mexico City's famous *Paseo de la Reforma*, and a lasting tribute to the unfortunate emperor.

Only three denominations of Mexican coins were made with the name and inscription of Maximilian. They were fashioned after French designs, and are rather attractive. Silver pesos and 50-centavo coins are available in a wide range of conditions at about $100 for Fine pieces up to $300 for Extremely Fine. Gold 20 pesos are very rare.

1.49x actual size

The Death Coin

MEXICO, CUENCAME. "MUERA HUERTA" SILVER PESO. 1914

No rare coin's high cost compares with the price one might have had to pay for owning one of the coins issued in Cuencame, Mexico, by Pancho Villa. In 1914, when Villa ordered the coins to be made, the country was engaged in widespread fighting for control by several factions, and the hatred between two of the parties was so intense that anyone caught holding one of Pancho Villa's coins could be shot on the spot. That was a pretty hefty price to pay for owning, or trying to spend, one of these coins, but in a sense it was somewhat justified.

Revolution plagued Mexico from 1910 to 1917 in a time of violence, confusion, and bloodshed. Four guerrilla leaders—Carranza, Obregón, Villa, and Zapata—fought each other, as well as trying to oust Victoriano Huerta, who had seized control of the Mexican government. Pancho Villa in particular hated Huerta for causing the death of ex-president Francisco Madero, who had started the revolution.

In an act of defiance and to further publicize his hatred for Huerta, Villa caused a silver peso to be made in 1914 at the mint in Cuencame, Durango. The design featured the symbolic Mexican eagle holding a snake on the obverse, and a liberty cap on the reverse. It also had the unique legend MUERA HUERTA—"Death to Huerta." This so incensed Huerta that he ordered the immediate execution of anyone found with one of the coins in his possession.

Historians disagree about what was right or wrong with the long and bloody Mexican revolution that resulted in Madero being overthrown and Huerta taking control of the country. Woodrow Wilson refused to recognize the new government, and the state existed under rebellion and terror with constant fighting in the northern states that were headed by Pancho Villa. The United States even dispatched troops to the port of Vera Cruz in 1914 to cut off the supply of arms. Pressure from the U.S., and other rebellions headed by Villa, caused Huerta to resign on July 15, 1914.

Throughout his career, Huerta had a long history of alcohol abuse, and Villa referred to him as *el Borrachito* or the Little Drunkard. In January 1916 he died of cirrhosis of the liver, thus ending the cruel but bright military career of a man who was a better general than a president.

Anyone caught holding one of Pancho Villa's coins could be shot on the spot. . . .

Pancho Villa and his ally Zapata continued to resist their rivals, Carranza and Obregón, and ultimately Villa was recognized as the legal head of Mexico's armed forces. However, the insurgent who had once commanded troop trains, artillery, and even an air force, was eventually reduced to what he had been at the beginning of the revolution: a poor marauder in the Chihuahuan sierra, filled with resentment against the American government that supported Carranza.

You will not have to pay with your life to own a specimen of the famous MUERA HUERTA coinage. Most pieces saw very little circulation and an Extremely Fine peso can now be purchased for about $300.

1.41x actual size

貴州省政府造
七錢二分

CHAPTER 8

Cathay and the Orient

Who Invented Coins?

China. "Spade" and "Knife" Money. First Millennium B.C.

There is little agreement about who made the first coins, or when or where they were made. Strong evidence points to the ancient merchants of Lydia, who very likely produced their famous electrum coins some time around 630 B.C. The coins they made were little more than lumps of metal that looked very much like raw placer gold that had been used as a valuable trade item in the past. The shape and form of these early coins were not very much different from those of today's money, and were part of an unbroken chain of development from ancient to modern times.

These coins were fashioned after familiar trade objects.

The early coins of China look quite different, and because of that they are sometimes overlooked as precursors to the development of money. In a sense they followed the same pattern as the Lydian coins: they were fashioned after familiar trade objects that had been used for many years. The hollow-handled "spade" coins were similar in shape to actual farm implements, and the "knife" coins were probably similar to knives or swords. There is no disagreement about the form of these coins, but there is wide divergence in an estimate of when they were made. "Sometime in the first millennium B.C." seems to be as close as anyone can deduce.

The best guess is that the copper spade coins were produced in China at about the same time that electrum coins were being made in Lydia. That two great cultures could come up with the same momentous

Small spade money.
(Actual size)

invention at the same time is not unique. More than one person envisioned the telephone, the television, the radio, and the airplane independently at nearly the same time. The range of 650 to 630 B.C. is probably as good a speculation as any for the beginning of coinage, and China may very well have been the originator. That country can also be given credit for later instigating the first decimal money, the first paper money, and the first mass-produced cast coinage.

All of the early Chinese coins were made of copper, considered a very valuable metal. The hollow-handled spade money looked like miniature farm implements, but was much too fragile to serve any purpose other than as a valuable trade item. In the years that followed, several symbolic variations in the shape of these coins were tried before the eventual round coins were made. Knife coins were made contemporaneously with the spades, or perhaps a little later. The first were approximately seven inches long, but later versions rarely exceeded five inches. All are much too fragile to have been used as cutting tools. They are moving reminders of the genesis of coins and money as one of the greatest benefits to humanity.

Early hollow-handled spade coins are scarce and not often available outside of Asia. They are also heavily counterfeited and difficult to authenticate. Genuine pieces usually have the handle opening packed with old dirt, and should be left in that condition. A Very Fine specimen will usually be priced at about $900. Smaller flat spade coins of the second and third century B.C. are often available at prices from $100 to $200. Old knife coins range in value from $500 to $1,000. Small "Ming" knives are priced at about $75.

Actual size

China's copper spade coins were produced at about the same time that electrum coins were being made in Lydia.

Actual size

A New Form of Money

China. Round Copper Coin of Yüan. Circa 250 B.C.

The round shape with a central hole mimics a very familiar Chinese design known as pi, *symbolizing Heaven.*

The ancient spade and knife coins of China must have been inconvenient to use in any normal transaction. They were large and bulky, with no easy way to transport or store them. This problem was partially overcome some time around the middle of the third century B.C., when a new form of coinage was introduced. There are no historical documents to confirm how, when, or where the new shape was chosen, but somehow it turned out to be round, and very much like the coinage of many other countries of that time except that they were cast in molds rather than being struck.

What is known is that for many years the early round coins of Yüan circulated concurrently with the traditional spade and knife coins in the western and eastern parts of China. It is also known that they were abolished by the first emperor of Ch'in when he unified the monetary system in 221 B.C. For all these reasons, the large early round coins of China are rather scarce today, and are highly sought after by collectors. One of their unique features is a round central hole. Nearly all later issues of round copper coins have square holes.

There is no easy explanation as to why a circular shape was chosen for these coins, or why their form was later changed to a smaller size with a square hole in the center. One theory is that the round shape was patterned after the end of the knife coins, which have a circular feature at the termination of the handle. It has been speculated that the circular end was retained while the bulky knife blade was discarded to make the coinage more convenient. Another theory holds that by the third century, coinage from other countries may have been seen and imitated in China. A more credible conjecture is that the round shape, with a round central hole, mimics a very familiar Chinese design known as *pi* (pronounced "bee"), symbolizing Heaven.

The pi is a popular shape that has been used in jewelry and decorative art for centuries. It is frequently seen, even today, carved in jade and attached to earrings or used as a hanging pendant or other accessory. The usual form is a thin flat disk with a round central hole, almost identical to the copper coin that is shown here to represent this phase in Chinese coinage.

Several different types of round coins were made during the short time that they were current in the third century B.C. The most common seems to be the Yüan type, with a single Chinese character on the right side of the round central hole. Ch'in, Yü, An-hsiang, and Chi-yin types are similar, but have additional characters and are much scarcer. Large early round Ming coins all have a square hole and are the most common coins of this era.

> Round copper coins of Yüan are elusive—especially genuine pieces, which are rarely seen. Those sold by street vendors in China are all modern imitations. The original pieces are thin and flat, with delicate characters and a hard patina. Originals generally sell for about $450 in any condition.

1.46x actual size

Turning Copper Into Gold

China. Wang Mang. Copper 5,000 Ch'ien "Knife" Money. A.D. 7

The Han Dynasty that had ruled in China since 206 B.C. was interrupted in 7 B.C. by minister Wang Mang, who usurped the throne by poisoning the young reigning emperor, P'ing Ti. Although never accepted as a legitimate emperor, Wang Mang did manage to stay in power until A.D. 22, and he did make a number of worthwhile changes in government affairs. Most notable was his attempt to reform the monetary system by introducing denominated token currency, and an official precious-metal coinage.

One of Wang Mang's early edicts declared all Han Dynasty coinage decrees null and void. He then proceeded to issue his own form of currency. Of his many unique designs, some coins were round, while others were sword shaped, and still others were rather like the late pu or spade coins. This later issue is among the most numerous of his unusual coins, and pieces were made in several denominations. The huo pu, or cloth money, pieces are the most common and are still readily available. Like many other old Chinese coins, they have been frequently counterfeited over the years and should be purchased only with caution.

The concept of a token coinage was very unusual in the first century B.C., and a daring innovation on the part of Wang Mang. Equally bold was his attempt to introduce precious-metal coins. Both concepts apparently failed to win popular support as most of these coins were only issued in limited quantities and are very rare today. The earliest of these reformed coins were the Chi Dao and Yi Dao knives. These knives in no way resemble their Zhou precursors; they look more like modern keys, or like cash coins attached to the end of a blade. The two types were valued at "500" and "5,000" cash respectively. Both are quite scarce and high on the want-lists of collectors of Asian coins.

The unusual Yi Dao knives are especially desirable because they show those words ("One Knife") incised in the metal and filled with gold. The gold inlay was added to give the coin a special appearance and perceived value that would make it worth its fiat value of 1,000 regular cash. Over the years many of these coins have been destroyed by the removal of their gold inlay. Others have had the round head removed to be spent like an ordinary coin. Still others on the market have been repaired by restoring any gold inlay that had been removed.

None of the denominated token-coins worked, and they were withdrawn in A.D. 14, and replaced by huo pu spade coins and round huo chuan cash. The reign of Wang Mang ended in 22 with a revolt that broke out in Szechwan province. With his death the Han authority was re-established and regular wu zhu coinage resumed.

> Wang Mang copper knife, or key, money is scarce and seldom available in the American marketplace. Authentication by an expert is mandatory before purchasing. Prices start at about $3,000 for any decent-looking example, and may reach double that for one in exceptional condition.

5,000-ch'ien "knife" (obverse). The gold inlay was added to give the coin a special appearance and perceived value. (Actual size)

Actual size

An Extremely Common Coin

China. Ch'ien-lung. Copper Cash. 1736–1795

Copper coinage in China was anything but uniform from the seventh century B.C. until the beginning of the first century A.D. After years of experimentation with odd shapes and types of coins, the ending rulers of the Han Dynasty adopted a more or less standardized form of a small coin called *ch'ien* or "cash." These coins were made of a lightly alloyed form of copper, and were round with a square central hole. The diameter varied, but was usually about one inch. Occasional deviations included multiple denominations, and emergency pieces made of lead or iron.

Emperor Ch'ien-lung's coins surely rank in quantity close to the U.S. Lincoln cent as the most common on Earth.

Identification of these coins consisted of four Chinese characters on the obverse, positioned at the top, bottom, right, and left side of the square central hole. The ruling emperor's name or reign title (*nien hao*) was placed at the top and bottom. Characters at the right and left were nearly always the same (*t'ung pao*), and indicated that this was valuable money. Production of these coins was carried out in foundries where large "trees" of 100 pieces were cast and then broken apart, filed, and finished by hand labor. It is said that punishment for counterfeiting was a lifetime sentence to work in the mints that produced these coins.

This form of money was used almost exclusively from the beginning of the first century until the introduction of machine-made coins in the late 1890s. To facilitate trade, the cash coins were strung in units of 100 and bundled in packages of 1,000. This ancient custom was likely the reason for the central hole in earlier times, and the reason it was continued for so long. The last of the cast cash coins was produced in 1912, at the beginning of the Chinese Republic.

Unimaginable quantities of Chinese cash coins were produced over the centuries in which they were the principal coin of the realm. If one were to speculate on what is the most common coin ever made, it would surely be the Chinese cash, and of all the similar-looking cash coins, those of Emperor Ch'ien-lung were the most prevalent. His coins surely rank in quantity close to the United States Lincoln cent as the most common coins on earth.

Throughout the years large quantities of Ch'ien-lung cash were melted, while others were used as decorations on sewing baskets in the 1930s, or strung to resemble dolls or short swords. Despite the millions of pieces that have been destroyed, these coins remain ubiquitous today, and have a deserving place in every collection.

Ch'ien-lung cash can be found in nearly every dealer's bargain box for about 25¢. They were produced in more than 20 different mints, each of which used a different mintmark on the reverse. Some of them are worth as much as $100. Search for the best condition possible (probably Extremely Fine), and expect to pay less than $2 for whatever you find.

2.4x actual size

Silver Shoes

CHINA. KUANG-HSÜ. SILVER SYCEE. CIRCA 1880

Commerce in China could not operate efficiently using only low-valued copper cash coins, or even with the omnipresent strings of 1,000 pieces (which traditionally contained only 970 coins at best). Large transactions were often conducted using silver in the form of ingots or castings of some special shape. The most popular of these were the so-called sycee ingots that were also called "boat" or "shoe" money. The name *sycee* is an English corruption of the Chinese *hsi-szu* (pronounced "see sue"), meaning "fine silk." The word refers to the thin wave-like casting lines seen on many of these pieces.

Sycee were made throughout China from the time of Kublai Khan, in the late 13th century, until the mid-1920s. Many emperors authorized the casting of sycee silver ingots in their names, while others were privately made or issued by merchants and banking houses. In 1856 the government recognized the sycee as official currency, and it remained so until the order was rescinded in 1933. During this time the sycee was the principal form of payment in wholesale business and customs duties. It was also used extensively in bank clearinghouses, in payment of taxes, and in salaries of government and municipal employees.

Throughout the centuries, many factors served to maintain the popularity of silver sycee among the Chinese. Because shoe money was usually about 98% pure silver it was a reliable monetary medium, and the weight was consistent within the district in which it was issued. Pieces were weighed in taels, and ranged in size from one tael (approximately one ounce) to 50. In contrast, coins and paper currency were extensively counterfeited, and the silver value of foreign coinage was difficult to calculate.

Many privately issued shoes or ingots were made for use as gifts and have the look of official pieces, but are usually stamped with characters wishing good luck or happiness. These were valued for their silver content, the same as sycee of other designs and shapes, and were accepted as currency after being tested and approved by a local bank or merchant.

With the civil disorders, revolutions, and invasions of the 20th century many wealthy Chinese converted their investments into silver sycee. Thousands of these popular silver shoes have gone into hiding and may be hoarded for generations to come. Others that escaped being accumulated, or being preserved by collectors, were sent to the melting pots during times when silver bullion was overvalued.

There are hundreds of different designs, shapes, and weights of these popular collectibles, but none as popular as the jumbo 50-tael pieces that contain nearly 50 ounces of pure silver. The recent appearance of many counterfeit sycee ingots makes it mandatory to have any contemplated purchases authenticated by an expert.

Thousands of these popular silver shoes have gone into hiding and may be hoarded for generations to come.

Shoe-shaped sycee are the most popular of the many types that are available. They are valued at about three times the price of silver bullion. Older pieces and those with odd shapes are often valued somewhat higher.

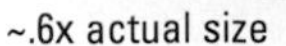

~.6x actual size

China, Yunnan Province, square 10-tael sycee. (Reduced)

An American Visit to Tokyo

JAPAN. TEMPO TSHUO. BRONZE 100 MON. CIRCA 1835

Commodore Matthew Perry was one of America's most prominent 19th-century historical figures. Known as the Father of the Steam Navy, he conducted the first school of naval gunnery, as well as being a hero in the Mexican-American War. It was no wonder that Perry was chosen to lead the world-shaking naval expedition to Japan in 1852 that led to foreign visitors finally being allowed to land in and trade with that country.

When Commodore Perry arrived in Japan he found a confusing system of hundreds of different kinds of gold, silver, and bronze coins.

Japan's hostile unwillingness to welcome outsiders was an effort to maintain independence and authority. Perry's successful negotiating paved the way for Japan to sign similar treaties with other Western nations, and ended the exotic Shogun era with its tyrannical warlords and samurai soldiers. It was the beginning of an industrial revolution that has made modern Japan a world leader in electronics, automobiles, and numerous other exports.

When Perry arrived he found the nation using a confusing assortment of hundreds of different kinds of gold, silver, and bronze coins. The coinage system was so diverse that merchants and bankers had to test most of the coins that passed their way, to determine metallic content and value. The large Japanese gold coins, called *oban*, were considered sacred and not allowed to leave the country. Normally both gold and silver coins were oblong bars, rather than round. The bronze coins, however, were patterned after the ch'ien from China, and consisted of round cast coins with a square central hole. In most instances the similar bronze coins of Japan, China, Korea, and Annam all passed interchangeably.

Commodore Perry took an interest in the money he saw in old Japan because he was a numismatist who had a collection of United States large cents, a variety of Greek and Roman coins, and many world coins that he had collected in his travels to foreign countries. Perry's collection passed to his daughter, Caroline Belmont, after his death in 1858, and was subsequently passed down from generation to generation until it was sold in 1994, and later dispersed at public auction in 1995. Among the many interesting coins that he found in Japan during his visits in 1853 and 1854 was a small hoard of oval-shaped Tempo Tshuo bronze 100-mon coins that were made around 1835.

These unusual coins are much larger than ordinary cash pieces, but feature the traditional central square hole. The inscription states that they were made during the Tempo era (1830–1843), and have the value of 100. The outer edge of each coin is stamped with a small cherryblossom punch mark. A quantity of 125 of these pieces was equal to one yen, or a Mexican dollar.

Fortunately for collectors, the impressive Tempo Tshuo 100-mon coins of Japan are still quite common and are readily available in Extremely Fine condition for less than $20. Those pedigreed to the Perry collection trade at $300.

Actual size

An Early Automobile in China

CHINA. KWEICHOW PROVINCE. SILVER DOLLAR. 1928

Modernization of Chinese coins began with machinery installed in the Canton Mint in 1890. Traditional bronze cash coins continued to be cast in foundries, but struck pieces valued at 5, 10, and 20 cash were also made concurrently. The new equipment made it possible to strike large silver dollar-size coins that were a staple item of trade throughout the country. From 1890 to the beginning of the Republic in 1912, numerous provincial mints produced silver coins that featured a symbolic dragon as the principal design. The large well-made Chinese dollar coins gradually replaced the Mexican pesos that had been used for decades.

The numerous variations on the dragon design that graces these coins make them a popular collectible. Coins of the Republic, issued 1912 to 1934, show a much greater variety of images and personalities. The lengthy series of Chinese dollars (a few were made as early as 1837) are of great interest to collectors because of their many designs, and could someday rival the avidly collected U.S. Morgan dollar series in their appeal.

The first Chinese dragon dollars weighed slightly more than foreign dollars that were in circulation. The difference made them immediately acceptable, but so many were hoarded that the weight was soon changed to make them equal to Mexican dollars. That weight standard was used thereafter for nearly all Chinese coins. The few exceptions are those occasional pieces denominated in taels instead of dollars.

Many of the designs are exotic, but few can compare with the silver dollar coins issued in Kweichow province in 1928, showing a motorcar as the central motif. At that time it was the first and only such design ever used on a coin, and was struck by order of governor Chow Hsi-chen, who was then in charge of Kweichow, to commemorate the opening of the first motor road in that province.

Adding to the intrigue of these coins is what seems to be a secret marking in the blades of grass beneath the automobile. They appear to be arranged to inconspicuously resemble the characters *si chen*, for Chow Hsi-chen's name. Whether he was bold enough to do such a thing remains a mystery, and a heated point of debate. Numerous variations in the auto design are known to exist, and serious collectors even count the number of spokes in the wheels, and the arrangement of lines in the ventilator, looking for minor varieties.

Another mystery surrounding this coin concerns exactly where it was made. Kweichow did not have a mint of its own before 1939, when parts of the Central Mint were shifted there from Shanghai as a wartime preservation measure. Yet this coin is inscribed with the name of Kweichow as the place or origin. As a collectible it is truly unique in many respects.

Adding to the intrigue of these coins is what seems to be a secret marking in the blades of grass beneath the automobile. . . .

Kweichow auto dollars have long been perennial favorites among collectors of world coins. It is difficult to locate one in condition higher than Extremely Fine, at about $2,500. A Very Fine specimen will cost $1,200 or more.

1.54x actual size

China's Last Emperor

CHINA. MARRIAGE DOLLAR OF P'U YI. 1923

P'u Yi, the last emperor of China, is known to numismatists through a limited number of coins made during his interrupted time in power that lasted from 1909 to 1912. He was only three years old when he left his family to live in the Forbidden City, where his father, Prince Ch'un, served as regent. An uprising in 1911 demanded a democratic form of government, forcing his resignation the following year. Six years after the revolution, a warlord named Chang Hsun made an unsuccessful attempted to restore P'u Yi to power.

The deposed emperor received limited schooling, but studied science, math, English, and other basic subjects. Supporters continued to hope that he would someday regain the throne, and provided him with an English tutor to educate him in Western ways. When he was 15 he tried to escape by bribing his guards, but the attempt was foiled when they betrayed him.

The wedding dollar's design contains a subtle joke that is easy to miss without careful examination. . . .

The few Chinese coins that have this emperor's reign title Hsuan Tung (his *nien hao*) consist of small cast copper cash pieces, some issues of silver dragon dollars, and in 1923, a silver dollar that was made to commemorate his marriage. He was only 16 when his advisors decided he should wed, and presented him with photographs of four eligible women from which to choose. His pick was a very beautiful girl of his own age, named Wan Jung, and later called Elizabeth. P'u Yi also took a Western name and was known as Henry for most of his life.

The silver dollar that commemorates this marriage probably never circulated widely, but it is considered a numismatic prize for its attractive design and its place in history. It also contains a subtle joke that is easy to miss without careful examination. Even though the legend reads "Made in the 12th year of the Republic of China," the basic theme is intended to restore the conventional dragon motif of the earlier Ching Dynasty.

On these coins the imperial dragon is replaced by a phoenix (Elizabeth) on the right and a dragon (Henry) on the left. Look carefully, and you will see that both are holding a glass of champagne to toast their wedding. It was a rather romantic beginning for a marriage that was soon to be torn asunder by unfortunate circumstances. P'u Yi had his share of customary concubines, and Elizabeth had an affair with a guard. She was confined to her rooms as punishment and eventually became mentally unstable and addicted to opium.

In 1931 the Japanese army invaded Manchuria and P'u Yi was proclaimed emperor. The Chinese government protested, and called P'u Yi a traitor for being a puppet of the Japanese occupiers. He later spent the rest of his life under house arrest in Japan, Russia, and finally China, where he died in 1967.

Dragon and Phoenix dollars of Henry P'u Yi are usually seen in high-grade condition as they received only very limited circulation. Pieces in Extremely Fine to About Uncirculated are typical, and will cost about $900. Uncirculated pieces trade at nearly double that amount.

1.54x actual size

Soviet China Dollars

China. Communist Dollar. 1934

The turmoil and changes brought about in China by the birth of the Republic were exacerbated by conflicts between those who would modernize the country; the traditionalists; and a communist movement akin to the Bolshevik Revolution. The communists began to operate independently as a party after the death of Sun Yat-sen in 1925. Josef Stalin believed that the communists should cooperate with the Kuomintang, while Leon Trotsky argued that the communists should begin establishing local governments within China. The followers of Stalin met their fiercest resistance from Mao Tse-tung and by 1928 Mao took control and established Soviet bases in Hunan and Kiangsi.

In 1931, Mao was elected chairman of the All-China Soviet Government, but he was unable to gain admission into the Chinese politburo, which remained in the hands of the Bolsheviks. The differences between the Bolsheviks and the Maoists were irreconcilable. Mao believed that land should be distributed to landlords and the poor alike; the Bolsheviks believed that the wealthy and the landlords should be deprived of all land. The campaign ended in defeating the Red Army and dislodging Mao from Kiangsi in mid-1934. The communists, however, were unhappy with any new leadership, and eventually restored Mao to power as head of the party.

During the many conflicts and struggles for control of the government, Soviet officials issued numerous coins in an effort to popularize their movement and bring a message of change to the people. The first were made in 1931, and then sporadically over the next three years. They were issued in several districts, and in many denominations in both copper and silver. The most notable of these are the large silver dollars that feature a hammer and sickle superimposed on a globe.

The legends on these coins are in Chinese but have a definite Soviet sentiment. They read, "Rise and Unite the Proletariat of the Whole World," "Chinese Soviet Republic," and "Made in the Szechuen-Shensi Provincial Mint." The date is most unusual because it is expressed (in Chinese) as the Christian-era year 1934, instead of traditional cyclical dating.

The propaganda effect of these coins was minimal and it was rumored at the time that anyone found using them could be subject to punishment for treason, and perhaps even death.

These coins are a poignant reminder of an important chapter in history that marked the beginning of communism in China. The Chinese Soviet Republic lasted until 1934, when the last of the communist party was driven from power. In 1949 the People's Republic of China was established and China emerged as an independent center of communist power.

It was rumored that anyone found using these coins could be subject to punishment for treason—perhaps even death.

There are numerous minor varieties of the Chinese Soviet silver dollars of 1933 and 1934. Extremely Fine specimens of the more common types sell for $500. Very Fine coins are usually offered for sale at about $300.

1.54x actual size

A Tael of Two Cities

Yunnan-Burma. Silver Tael. Circa 1943

This is a mysterious and controversial coin if there ever was one. Specimens first appeared outside the Orient around 1963 and have been a source of consternation ever since. At first they were thought to have been made for use somewhere in Yunnan Province and bordering Burma. Speculation was that they might have been used to pay workers maintaining the famous Burma Road during World War II. The road was an important link between Burma and China, and used by the British to transport war materials to China before Japan intervened. These coins have also been often attributed to Laos because of their bilingual inscription. Most modern researchers, however, now agree that they were struck in Hanoi under official direction from the Colonial Vichy Finance Department, and used as currency for purchases in Laos and Tonkin.

The variety shown here was probably made in 1943 or 1944. The denomination is shown as one tael, (or *liang*). A very similar half-tael coin has the same design and inscription. The obverse design has the Chinese character *Fu,* meaning "wealthy." A second variation on this coinage shows a stag head as the design on the obverse, and similar bilingual wording ("Pure Silver / One Tael") on the reverse. Only one-tael coins were made with the stag design. The pieces contained one Chinese *liang* of pure silver, which is roughly equivalent to one ounce.

These bullion pieces now seem to have originated in Hanoi during World War II. The opium monopoly of the French colonial government, which sold opium to the people of Indochina and Cochinchina, no longer had a supply of silver coins to pay the hill tribes of Vietnam and Laos for the raw opium. Still, they would not relinquish their opium monopoly because it was a major source of revenue. Silver from many sources was gathered and made into these coins that quickly found their way to the hill tribes. From there they were mostly melted and made into jewelry or silver bars.

When World War II ended, the United Nations assigned the Nationalist Chinese government to control the Japanese surrender in the northern half of Indochina (Laos and Vietnam). During that time much silver, along with other valuables, was taken from the hill tribes and brought to China. It is assumed that many of these coins that are now attributed to French Indochina were among the loot, and have likely been melted or destroyed since then.

Yunnan-Burma stag-head tael, 1943. (.75x actual size)

These curious "opium" coins are popular collectible items, and not at all common. The fu type one-tael pieces are usually available in Uncirculated condition for about $175. Half-tael coins of the same type sell at $100. Stag-head pieces are a bit scarcer and difficult to locate in choice Uncirculated condition, but still trade at under $225. The design is often weakly struck on all of these coins.

1.5x actual size

A Unique Form of Money

China. Tai Ping Rebellion. Silver One-Quarter Tael. Circa 1860

In the mid-19th century, the use of opium spread far and wide throughout China, giving birth to several rebellions. The Tai Ping rebellion, which killed more than 20 million people, was a revolution against opium and for a communist-Christian form of government. When Shanghai was threatened by this movement, foreign interests organized an army and helped the corrupt imperial Manchu forces to crush the Tai-pings. From 1851 to 1864 the country suffered from the rebellion, led by Hong Xiuquan, a visionary who had been influenced by a dream and felt that he was called to rid China of idolatry and corruption.

Hong set out to overthrow the Manchu government and replace it with his own kingdom called *Tai Ping*, meaning "Great Peace," but as the warring went on the movement lost much of its Christian emphasis. Hong became obsessed with the idea that he was a brother with Jesus Christ, and fated to rule all of China. After establishing his capital in Men Ging, his armies extended their control over large areas of the country.

The "Heavenly Kingdom of Great Peace" (*T'ai P'ing T'ien Kuo*) issued a number of cast bronze cash coins. These are very similar to all other cash pieces, with the familiar round shape and square hole in the center. All are scarce and many are rare, although they must have been plentiful at the time and saw wide circulation. Their scarcity today can be attributed to widespread destruction of everything that was associated with the Tai Ping movement at the end of the war. When the rebel capital, Nanking, was captured by imperial troops in 1864, the slaughter was beyond belief. The general in charge of the operation reported to the emperor that not one of the rebels surrendered and every one had to be killed. More than 100,000 were murdered in that city alone, and some parts of the country were so badly depopulated that the effects were still felt at the turn of the century.

During the brief glory days of the Tai Ping Kingdom, they issued not only bronze cash coins, but also a unique form of silver coinage. These were in denominations of one-half and one-quarter tael. Each coin was individually hand engraved with the characters *T'ien Kuo* ("Heavenly Kingdom") on the obverse, and *Sheng Pao* ("Sacred Currency") on the reverse. There is no explanation as to why the labor-intensive hand-engraving technique was used to produce these coins. The production must have been limited, and perhaps the coins were used only for very special purposes. The few remaining pieces in collections today confirm that they were never very common.

A survey of private collections and museums reveals that only about two dozen of these exceptional coins are still in existence. Six of these are one-quarter tael pieces; the others are one-half tael coins. They fill a place in world history and numismatic lore rivaled by few other coins.

It is difficult to place a value on these rare coins. Few exist outside of museums, and none has been sold in recent years. Past sales have been in the range of $2,500 to $3,500.

Hong became obsessed with the idea that he was a brother with Jesus Christ, and fated to rule all of China. . . .

2.15x actual size

GETTO
1943

CHAPTER 9

Emerging Concepts in Coinage

When Was It Made?

The Netherlands. Philip the Good. Silver Briquet. 1484

Acquiring one of these rare and historically important coin varieties is a major numismatic event.

Dates of one sort or another have been used on coins since 312 B.C. when the Seleucids marked their coins according to an era commencing when they regained possession of Babylon. Other ancient states began using various forms of dating during the third century B.C. These usually counted years from the time a ruler came into power, or from the founding of a city. Unfortunately, most ancient coins can only be roughly dated based on style and fabric, or by historical evidence.

A greater uniformity in dating was achieved around A.D. 525 when reckoning from the birth of Christ was calculated by a Scythian monk, Abbot Dionysius Exigius. The concept spread rapidly throughout Europe, but was used mostly for record keeping and official documents. The thought of adding dates to coins would not occur until many years later, and even the length of each year was subject to occasional revision before the Gregorian calendar was settled on in 1582. While a majority of today's world coins are dated in the Christian cycle, that system is by no means exclusive. A great many other cyclical systems are used by individual countries and religious groupings.

The first coin known to use a Christian date appears to be a small silver denier made in Roskilde, Denmark, in 1234. The inscription on this amazing coin reads M:CC:XXX:IIII on the obverse, around a bishop's cap. The reverse reads ANNO DOMINI, around what seems to be a church. A scant half dozen of these coins are know to exist, and probably none of them are outside of museums. It would be another 138 years before any other coin took up the dating custom, and that was only briefly, from 1372 to 1375, when Roman-numeral dates were used on silver groschen from Aachen. Like the earlier examples, these coins are all extremely rare and unavailable to collectors.

Dated coins began to be more commonplace beginning around 1484, when several Central European countries added markings to their money. Roman numerals were frequently used, but original forms of Arabic numerals were also tried. By 1500 the act of dating European coins became customary, and soon spread around the world. One hundred years later nearly all coins began to use dates to express continuity in coinage and mark when and where each piece of money was made. The innovation helped to verify the stability and value of a coin by establishing when and by whom it was authorized.

Collectors view the category of pre-1500 dated coins as a special numismatic grouping that engenders interest and reverence because all are rare and historically important. Acquiring any one of the several different varieties of these coins is a major event as they seldom appear on the market.

All of the pre-1500 dated coins should be considered rare and desirable, but they are not all tremendously expensive. Some go unnoticed because of the difficulty in reading the dates. A typical example will probably cost around **$300**.

2.50x actual size

Ducats from Venice

Venice. Doge Antonio Venerio. Gold Ducat. 1382–1400

The gold ducats of Venice are some of the most well-known and significant coins in history. They were first made in 1284, and continued to be issued for several hundred years by successive doges of the city. The coins are made of pure gold and weigh approximately 3.5 grams. Most are 21 mm in diameter, with but slight variance over the years. All are uniform in design: the obverse depicts St. Mark standing at the left, with the doge kneeling at the right, holding a banner alongside which is the word DUX. On the reverse is the figure of Christ, surrounded by stars.

The word *ducat* was first applied to the silver grossi of Venice, but later came to be used exclusively for the gold coins. The coins were so highly respected that they saw use throughout Europe and as far east as India. The method of coining this gold was not changed throughout their history; they were all hand-hammered, and made of the purest gold available. The issue of ducats essentially ended with the dissolution of the Venetian Republic in 1797, long after most other mints were using mechanical coinage equipment.

Early in the 15th century the word *ducat* began to displace the Florentine *florin* as the common expression for a gold coin. Coins of similar size and weight soon began to be issued in France, Germany, Bohemia, Hungary, and even in Florence. The place of the Venetian gold ducat thus earned its reputation as being one of the most influential and sought-after coins ever minted. Fortunately for collectors these attractive gold coins are still widely dispersed and readily available at modest prices.

In Shakespeare's time the ducat of Venice was well known as a coin of value, and the term was widely used in several of his plays. In *Romeo and Juliet,* we read, "I see that thou are poor; Hold, there is forty ducats." The ducat is also mentioned in *Hamlet*: "Those that would make mows at him while my father lived give twenty, forty, fifty, a hundred ducats apiece for this picture in little." In *The Comedy of Errors* we find, "The fineness of gold, and changeful fashion, which doth amount to three and odd ducats more than I stand debted to this gentleman." The word *ducat* has become so entrenched in theater jargon that it has somehow become a modern slang expression for a ticket.

These coins are probably best remembered for their central role in *The Merchant of Venice*, where they are mentioned several times. And visitors to Venice will also remember seeing them among the street vendors' stalls in the Piazza of San Marco.

Many of the Venetian ducats made by the numerous doges over the years are relatively common and valued at about $500 for a piece in Very Fine to Extremely Fine condition. Expect to pay more for one at a stall in Venice, but you can be confident that it will quite likely be genuine.

"But fare thee well. There is a ducat for thee."
—The Merchant of Venice. II. iii. 4.

2.86x actual size

A Coin from the Valley

Bohemia. Joachimsthal. Silver Thaler. Circa 1500

From a rich German valley came the coin that would transform into the American dollar. . . .

It is generally recognized that the English word *dollar* is an adaptation or corruption of the German word *thaler*. The source of the German term is a bit more obscure. The story of the origin of this term is an interesting chapter in the evolution of numismatic nomenclature and is closely related to the American dollar.

In 1432, the emperor Sigismund of Bohemia granted to Jasper Schlick the rank of count. Knowing that extensive silver deposits had been discovered on Schlick's two estates of Michelsberg and Joachimsthal, Sigismund also granted him the right to coin money. When Schlick died without issue, these rights passed to his brother Matthew. Finally, in 1517, Matthew's four grandsons found the silver mines even richer than had been expected and began to coin large pieces of money. These were generally called *Joachimsthaler Gueldengroschen*, or "Gueldengroschen from the Valley of St. Joachim."

The Schlick coins were of exceptional quality and fineness, and won sufficient acceptance so that their name was in time applied to all similar large coins. The awkwardly long title was eventually contracted to *Joachimsthaler* and later to *thaler*. Thus the modern dollar is, etymologically, a coin from the valley.

This original thaler merits a brief description. The obverse bears the legend LVDOVICVS PRIM D GRACIA REX BO, meaning "Louis I by the Grace of God King of Bohemia." A crowned Bohemian lion is shown in profile as the central design. On the reverse is a full-length

1.5x actual size

standing figure of Saint Joachim holding a staff. At his feet is the family coat of arms of the counts of Schlick.

The early Joachimsthalers were made for many years in their original form, and later many other districts and countries imitated them. They were widely accepted because of their convenient large size and purity of silver. As the first silver dollar-size coins ever produced, they set the stage for what eventually became the most popular coins in the world. In the Netherlands a similar coin became known as a *rijksdaalder*, in Denmark *rigsdaler*, in Italy *tallero*, in Poland *talar*, and in Sweden *daler*.

All of the above names were variations on the denomination and names *Joachimsthaler, thaler,* or *taler*. In Spain and in the British American colonies the 8-reales coin became known as a *dollar*, and was the precursor in size and name of our American dollar. The designation was officially adopted as the standard monetary unit of the United States by Congress on July 6, 1785.

Bohemian *Joachimsthalers* of any date or design are scarce. The original issues of Count Schlick sell for about $2,500 in Very Fine condition. Those of his descendents, with different designs similar to the piece shown here dated 1556, are worth between $500 and $1,000.

The large silver coins of the Netherlands, Italy, Poland, and many other countries would all inherit their names from the thaler. . . .

(Top to bottom) Netherlands leuwendaalder (lion dollar); Saxony taler; Italy talero; United States dollar. (Actual size)

Paper Coins

The Netherlands, Leyden. Paper 5 Sols. 1574

Whoever first said that money does not grow on trees did not know about the strange paper coins of the Netherlands that were made in 1574. The Netherlanders were the first—and perhaps the only—people to ever try using paper as a substitute for metal coins. They made what many consider to be true coins, not simply paper money as we know it today. Actually, these unusual pieces are fiat tokens or emergency money made as a substitute for the real thing at a time when no silver was available.

Silver for making coins was non-existent during the siege, so a sort of papier-mâché was made from old books, including prayer books and Bibles.

The event occurred in the city of Leyden when two provinces of the Netherlands, Holland and Zeeland, were under attack by Spanish forces. The paper coins made by the city of Leyden are called "siege money" by numismatists, who include them in a broad category of emergency money made by numerous cities while under siege or during wartime. Other similar pieces have been made of brass, wood, melted cannons, and even cut-up pieces of silver tableware, but Leyden was the only city to use paper. (In a more recent example of emergency money, in 1943, during World War II, the United States resorted to using zinc-coated steel as a substitute for copper in one-cent coins.)

King Philip of Spain (1556–1598) made a great number of campaigns in an effort to maintain Spanish superiority and spread the Catholic faith. His main conflict was against the Dutch rebels in the Netherlands' War of Independence from 1567 to 1648. The campaign in Flanders in 1574, with the battle of Mook and the siege of Leyden, resulted in Spanish victory over the Protestant leaders at Mook, but defeat at the city of Leyden. The cost of that victory was a testament to the tenacity and ingenuity of the citizens who defended the city with every ounce of their strength.

During the siege all supplies to the city were cut off from May to October in 1574. Food was carefully rationed, but soon the city was reduced to near starvation. Silver for making coins was non-existent, so to facilitate local needs a sort of papier-mâché was made from old books, including some prayer books and Bibles. Disks were made the same size as their traditional 5- and 20-stiver coins, and stamped with coinage dies. The pieces look very much like the silver coins, except they are made of paper rather than metal.

The siege was finally broken in October when the surrounding countryside was flooded and ships were able to reach the city with supplies and relief. There are no records telling what became of the emergency money after the siege was lifted, but some must have been saved as reminders of the hardships of this terrible event. After the war, Leyden was offered a reward of exemption from taxation, but instead chose to have a university built in the city. The victory is still celebrated with a festival in the Netherlands on October 3 each year.

Specimens of Leyden paper siege money are difficult to locate and are rarely offered for sale. Most are in Very Fine condition and are worth about $1,000 today.

1.90x actual size

To Coin a Phrase

Venice. Copper Gazzetta. Circa 1650

Money terms are used in everyday expressions with little thought about their origin. "Filthy lucre," "put in your two cents," "pin money," "a sawbuck," "passing the buck"—all are common phrases related to money. Collectors like to reflect on what they mean and how they entered the English language. Some are obscure, some are self-evident, others have interesting backgrounds. One that is frequently overlooked is the derivation of the word *gazette*, often used as the name of a newspaper.

Few people know that today's *gazette* comes from a Venetian coin of the 17th century. The coin was a 2-soldi copper piece that was called a "gazzetta." This was a diminutive of the Latin word *gaza*, meaning "treasure." These coins are about one inch in diameter and have the lion of Venice surrounded by the words SAN MARC VEN *II* on the obverse, and DALMA ET ALBAN on the reverse.

Shortly after the gazzetta was first made for circulation, Venice commenced to publish an official newspaper dealing with public affairs. The paper sold to the citizens for one gazzetta, and before long the paper itself became known as the gazzetta. The name stuck and has become synonymous with publications ever since.

The term *buck*, meaning a dollar, has its origin with the American Indians and early settlers who valued deerskins as a medium of exchange. A *copperhead* was a person in the Northern states who sympathized with the South during the Civil War, and got the name from the Civil War tokens that were made of copper and used extensively in the North. The word *jitney*, for a small bus, was originally a token, and later the British coin that was the price of a fare.

"Weird as a three-dollar bill" got its reputation when the government first made greenback bills in 1861 but neglected to make an anticipated note of that denomination. When the public learned that there was no such thing, anything odd or unusual was compared to the non-existing money. *Pin money* was originally tattered and repaired paper money of colonial America that was given to a housewife to spend for household items. It was often so worn that it had to be sewn or held together with pins, and unworthy of use by the man of the house.

In England the admonition "Spend a penny" means do not be frugal—just do it and spend the money. The expression originated with the public toilets that charged a penny toll to open the lock on the doors. "Another day, another dollar" meant just that in the early 20th century, when wages in America were one dollar for a day's work.

"Another day, another dollar" was meant literally in the early 1900s.

Examples of these interesting coins are not expensive. The Venetian copper gazzetta shown here can be found with some hunting and should cost no more than $50. A genuine old buckskin will cost considerably more.

2.14x actual size

Money by the Pound

Sweden. Copper Plate Money. One Daler. 1736

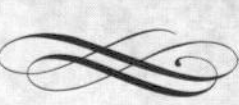

King Gustavus Adolphus called Sweden's debt "the consuming cancer of the country."

The Kalmar War was a struggle between Sweden and Denmark for supremacy in the Baltic. It raged from 1611 to 1613. In 1612, Sweden lost the fortress of Alvsborg and its only access to the Baltic, but this did not ensure success to the Danes under Christian IV, and he was never able to conquer Sweden itself. When the Dutch and the Hanseatic League joined with Sweden, Christian was forced to sue for peace. In January 1613, the war ended in a draw with the signing of the Treaty of Knared. The Swedes, however, had to pay a ransom for the return of Alvsborg, in the amount of a million riksdalers specie, within a period of six years.

King Gustavus Adolphus of Sweden called the payment of this debt "the consuming cancer of the country," and when it was finally paid the country was exhausted of silver to such a degree that even the table silver of the king had to be sent to the mint and melted. At the same time the local silver mines were being depleted, and thus the copper mine at Falum became an increasingly important resource. With little silver for national coinage, the king turned to his copper wealth as a solution to the financial crisis.

In 1644 a daring experiment was tried using huge plates of copper in place of silver coins. The first of these was a gigantic 10-daler piece weighing nearly 45 pounds that was made only during that year. Then in 1649 production was resumed, this time with 8-daler pieces being the largest, at 12" x 24". The 4-daler pieces measured 10" x 10", the 2-daler coins 7" x 8", 1-daler pieces about 5" x 7", and 1/2 daler, the lowest denomination, 4"x 4".

Frequent production of these pieces continued until 1759, which was the last date used, although some were made until 1776 using dies of earlier years.

Actual size

Manufacture of these unusual slabs involved rolling, hammering, and cutting strips of copper into "plates," and then stamping them in the center and in each corner with markings similar to those of coinage dies. The inscription SILF MYNT indicates these are to be considered "silver money" and valued as such.

The copper mine at Falum was very productive and brought a good profit to the kingdom, especially after the copper plate money was proclaimed legal tender. Yet, the bulky pieces were always inconvenient and difficult to use. To overcome this difficulty the government began an issue of paper credit notes, the first ever outside of China, to be used as a substitute for the plates. In time, the paper money became better accepted, and certainly more convenient than the plate money, and the concept of promissory notes backed by gold, silver, or even copper, soon spread around the world.

Today, 8- and 10-daler plates are nearly unobtainable. Four-daler pieces sell for about $2,000; 2-daler plates at $1,000; 1-daler plates are valued at about $800; and 1/2-daler plates bring around $350. Sea-corroded pieces from sunken ship recovery sell for about half those amounts.

The first of these plates was a gigantic 10-daler piece weighing nearly 45 pounds.

Actual size

A Taxing Tradition

RUSSIA. COPPER BEARD TAX TOKEN. 1705

Peter the Great of Russia carried out many changes during his long and stormy reign (1689 to 1725). He built the magnificent city of St. Petersburg, laid the foundation of a native industrial system, and expanded commerce with the West. Through these reforms he hoped to add Western ways to the conservative mode of his country. Upon returning from a trip to Europe, he decreed that his Russian citizens should dress like Europeans, specifically in the German fashion, and shave their patriarchal beards. It was his belief that these reforms would inspire a deeper appreciation of the culture of Europe and change the outmoded ways of Russia.

The czar decreed that Russian citizens should dress like Europeans, and shave their patriarchal beards. . . .

His proposals met with immediate and strong resistance. The boyars reminded the czar that a bearded man was the image and likeness of God, and that to shave was blasphemy. Even the lower aristocracy found shaving offensive, and forced a mediation of the edict. The czar agreed to a compromise in which anyone not complying with the law could avoid it by paying a substantial tax for the privilege of preserving his facial hair.

In 1705 special "beard tax tokens" were minted, and given to those who paid the tax. The design on these copper coin-like pieces is unique. On the obverse is the imperial crowned double-headed eagle above the Russian words for "1705 Year," all within a circular wreath of small laurel leaves. The reverse has a Russian legend translated as "Money Token," and below that is a nose, moustache, lips, and a beard, all within a circular wreath of laurel leaves. Near the left edge there is a small oval counterstamp with a double-headed eagle.

The czar's campaign to make his subjects look more like Westerners decreed that persons of every class, except priests and deacons, should shave, but that those who did not want to shave should pay an annual tax. The tax ranged from 30 to 100 rubles, for the various classes of nobles, landowners, and officials. A flat rate of two dengi (one kopeck) per beard was established for peasants. Those who paid the tax were given a tax token to carry as proof of payment and entitlement to wear a beard or moustache.

Only tokens dated 1705 are known to exist, and it is not known if the edict extended for more than one year. It is possible that the counterstamp found on these pieces may have been a re-validation mark for a subsequent year, but no records remain to confirm this theory. Twenty-four years later, long after Peter's death, a review of the edict was ordered by Empress Elizabeth concerning the hated custom of Western dress and enforced shaving. In consideration of the failure of the project, restrictions were lifted in 1762, but by then many of Russia's city dwellers had already conformed to Western customs.

Most of the despised beard tax tokens were destroyed after they went out of use. They are now rare and seldom offered for sale. Very Fine specimens sell easily for $1,500.

2.5x actual size

Merchants to the Rescue

England. Copper Token Halfpenny. 1794

In the late-18th century, commerce in England was hampered by a serious shortage of small change. Copper coins had not been made for circulation from 1754 to 1770, and after that only for the years 1770 to 1775. The situation was made even worse by an enormous number of lightweight counterfeit copper coins made from old coins taken from circulation. The public was left without means of paying for low-value items, and merchants were forced to use their ingenuity to find ways to make change.

From 1792 to 1797, merchants resorted to issuing their own token money in order to do business. The tokens they made not only were profitable for them, but also could carry advertising or other messages. By 1794, hundreds of businesses, in districts all over England, were issuing their own individually designed tokens. The themes and imagery on these pieces are as varied as those who made them. Some carry straightforward advertising, while others are political or even satirical. The great variety of designs used on these tokens has made them popular favorites among collectors ever since they were first made more than 300 years ago.

Some of the more popular depictions include a piece from Coventry showing Lady Godiva riding on her horse, and those showing other noteworthy historical figures and buildings. Pieces related to Thomas Paine and to the Franklin Press are of interest to American collectors, while those showing various strange animals in the Pidcocks' Circus appeal to everyone. The most enigmatic of all, and a favorite with collectors everywhere, is a piece from Middlesex that contains an entertaining rebus.

The outer inscription on this piece is straightforward: A MAP OF FRANCE 1794. The inner design is contained within a border of daggers, and shows various symbols, words, and a human foot. The rebus has been interpreted as follows: "There is fire in every corner; the country is surrounded by danger (daggers); Honor is underfoot; France is divided (shown as FRA-NCE); the throne is overturned; Glory is erased; and Religion (RE\LI/GI\ON) is all broken up." On the other side of this token is the fervent wish, MAY GREAT BRITAIN EVER REMAIN THE REVERSE.

The lengthy series of provincial tokens has fascinated collectors ever since the first comprehensive book on the subject was published by the Rev'd James Conder in 1798. Early interest resulted in many pieces being made especially for collectors. A variety of interesting and unusual designs, and combinations of dies, produced thousands of pieces that are now enjoyed by collectors, and generally called "Conder tokens."

Hundreds of common English tradesmen's tokens are available in Extremely Fine to Uncirculated condition at prices from $50 to $200. Rare varieties and popular designs may cost from $250 to several thousand dollars. Common Very Fine or worn pieces are generally valued at $20 to $30 each.

A popular halfpenny token from Coventry, showing Lady Godiva riding on her horse. (Actual size)

1.96x actual size

A Thought for Your Penny

Britain. Copper "Cartwheel" Penny. 1797

The shortage of small change that plagued England at the end of the 18th century was a concern to the government as well as for merchants and buyers. Numerous private tokens and lightweight counterfeit pieces served out of necessity, but were more of an annoyance than a solution. Eventually, it took private industry to come up with a plan to remedy the situation.

In June of 1797, Matthew Boulton, who previously had made private merchant tokens, was given a royal commission to strike official copper coins at his mint in Soho. Boulton's establishment was far more technically advanced than the Royal Mint, and he had demonstrated that his products would be better in every respect than any previous coins. His strategy was to use steam power, as had recently been perfected by his business partner, James Watt. Excellence of design and speed of production were the keys to their success, securing approval to proceed with their coinage program.

A box cleverly crafted from a 1797 "cartwheel" twopence. (Reduced)

The coins that Boulton produced, unlike any in the past, were perfectly round, with a finely engraved portrait of the king and neatly formed lettering. They also had a raised border around the edge, with incuse letters and date. Two different denominations of copper coins were produced: the 1-penny piece that is 36 mm in diameter and weighs exactly one ounce; and the 2-penny piece at 41 mm, weighing exactly two ounces. Both were larger, thicker, and heavier than any copper coins of the past, and they soon received the nickname of *cartwheels* because of their size. The term has remained with them ever since, and is still used by coin collectors.

The new coins received a mixed reaction when first placed in circulation. The penny was well received, but the bulky twopence coins were apparently too clumsy for easy use, and they were made only in limited quantity during 1797. In an effort to encourage circulation, a rumor was spread stating that some of the twopence coins had been hollowed out and a five-pound note was enclosed inside. The rumor touched off a wave of testing the coins by knocking their edges to see if they might pop open and reveal a hidden treasure. The end result was that the vast majority of these coins have edge dents. Collectors have come to expect these marks and tend to overlook them as blemishes because they are more a part of the charm and lore of these coins.

Boulton's oversized coins have left another legacy that has lasted until modern times. Because of their precise weight they have long been used to make minor adjustments to the mechanism that controls the accuracy of the famous Big Ben clock in Parliament Tower in London.

Cartwheel pennies are all dated 1797 but were probably made for several years afterwards. They are relatively common in Very Fine grade and sell for about $30. Uncirculated pieces are priced at $350. Twopenny pieces are scarcer and in high demand, with Very Fine at $100, and Extremely Fine at $300.

1.67x actual size

A Coin Fit for a Queen

Austria. Maria Theresa. Silver Taler. 1780

If a contest were held to choose the world's most popular coin, the winner might well be the famous Maria Theresa taler of Austria. This coin has the unique distinction of having been used as money throughout the world for the past 200 years. The reason for this popularity is that these coins contain a full weight of silver that has never been lessened or altered in any way. Neither the size, nor the design, nor the date has been changed since these coins were first made in 1780. They hold a record that is matched by few other coins in history.

Because of the longevity and popularity of this coin it is in constant demand by collectors all over the world. Its beauty appeals to many. Others are fascinated by the lovely Austrian coat of arms, and the 1780 date that still appears on the reverse. In one survey of collector interest, the Maria Theresa taler was voted as one of the world's most beautiful coins. While that title may be debated, it is undisputed that the design is realistic, well balanced, and attractive.

The portrait of Empress Maria Theresa shows her in the year of her death: a moment that has been frozen in time as a tribute to this great woman. Her full title around the border proclaims that she was Empress of the Holy Roman Empire, Queen of Hungary and Bohemia, Archduchess of Austria, Duchess of Burgundy, and Countess of Tyrol. She was truly royal, and one of the greatest women in history. Maria Theresa was a staunch champion of science and medical research, and instituted many reforms aimed at making life more endurable for the poor. Her friendships with Madame Pompadour and Catherine the Great did much to enhance the role of women in 18th-century Europe. She was the mother of 16 children, many nearly as famous as she—one daughter, Marie Antoinette, married King Louis XVI of France.

In the past these large coins were used as money in various countries that did not have their own mints. Traders who recognized the design would not allow any alterations or substitutes. Thus, the coins have come down to us unchanged since 1780. Over the years these pieces have been made intermittently at many world mints, but since 1860 coinage has been restricted to Austria, where they were originally minted.

Each of these coins contains a little more than 28 grams of .833 fine silver. They are slightly larger than U.S. silver dollars and, like them, contain more than three-quarters of an ounce of pure silver. The edge has a special design with lettering that is used only on these coins.

Maria Theresa was truly royal, and one of the greatest women in history. . . .

> Beautiful, well-made specimens of the Maria Theresa taler have been made throughout the past 50 years. Much older pieces are apt to be not as well struck. Uncirculated coins are generally priced only slightly above silver bullion value. Proof specimens are generally available under $20.

1.5x actual size

The Alchemist

Nicaragua. The Bandit Sandino. 10 Gold Pesos. 1928

For centuries, the physical goal of the alchemist was the transmutation of gold from base metals such as lead and copper. The Philosopher's Stone of the Wise was said to confer the ability to create gold, prolong life, and cure all diseases. With it, the Elixir of Immortality could be obtained. With these aspirations in mind, it is no wonder that the ancient art of alchemy has persisted even to modern times, despite continual failure. There was a single man, however, who did succeed, in a sense, by making his own version of gold coins out of lead.

While Sandino may have succeeded in making his lead coins pass for gold, the entire episode was a terrible tragedy.

The ingenious alchemist was General Agusto César Sandino. He was a revolutionary leader in Nicaragua who led the United States Marines on a merry chase up and down the country in 1928 and 1929 in his fight against the conservative government headed by Adolfo Díaz and Emiliano Chamorro. Sandino protested against the U.S. intervention in Nicaragua in 1926 and the elections of 1927, and formed a guerrilla campaign against the occupying Marines sent there to restore order. No minor character, he led a sizable resistance army of jungle fighters equipped with rifles and machine guns.

The bandit army had to re-provision from time to time, and resorted to raiding local stores for all their needs. The general felt obligated to pay for his supplies, but without money he decided on a plan that would leave the frightened storekeepers with some compensation. After gaining control of the American-owned San Albino gold mines (located in the northern part of the country), some say he made a few gold coins, although none are known today. He then removed the lead water pipes from the mine and used that base metal to make more coins with the same molds.

The Sandino lead coins are inscribed R. DE. N. 10 PESOS ORO (*oro* meaning "gold") on the obverse, and INDIOS DE A. C. SANDINO on the reverse. It is believed that fewer than six or seven of these unusual coins have survived, although at least two different dies were used to make them. The variety shown here, with a retrograde dollar sign before the denomination, is unique. These pieces are slightly larger than a quarter dollar and about three times as thick, and are crudely cast and barely legible.

While Sandino may have succeeded in making his lead coins pass for gold, the entire episode was a terrible tragedy. He made a practice of inspecting the villages, and if he did not find his money in circulation, he would kill the "offenders." If the Marines and the National Guard found people with the coins, they too might kill them, as suspected rebels. The bandit slipped back and forth into Honduras, eluding capture, but finally ended his reign of terror after the U.S. Marines withdrew. He was seized and executed in 1934.

The coins of Sandino are rather obscure and considered to be unauthorized tokens or emergency money, rather than an official issue of Nicaragua. Few have ever been traded on the numismatic market, and there are no recent valuations.

2x actual size

Money to Burn

Poland. Lodz Ghetto. 10 Mark. 1943

In September 1939, Adolph Hitler, chancellor of Nazi Germany, viciously attacked neighboring Poland. Unable to withstand his blitzkrieg tactics, Poland fell within three weeks. At that time, the city of Lodz, located in central Poland, held the second largest Jewish community in Europe—smaller only than Warsaw's—and when the Nazis attacked, Poles Christian and Jewish worked together to defend their city. Seven days after the attack began, Lodz was occupied, and the Jews became immediate targets for beatings, robberies, and unlawful seizure of their property.

At the time of the occupation, Lodz had a Jewish population of 230,000. Their immediate incarceration was ordered, and an internment camp was hastily set up to contain them. The Nazis did not just stop with having the Jews locked up in a small area; they wanted them to pay for their own food, security, sewage removal, and all other expenses of their containment. A single person, Mordechai Chaim Rumkowski, was placed in charge of managing the entire ghetto.

Rumkowski was a firm believer in the autonomy of the ghetto and he attempted to establish programs that would generate revenue to help pay for living expenses. He replaced the German currency with ghetto money, and paid workers for their contributions to the community. The efforts were far too little to sustain the needs of such a large population, and starvation and hardships were widespread. Still the Nazis continued to insist that the ghetto pay for its own upkeep, and drained the population of all their resources.

Special coins were made for use within the ghetto. These consisted of 5-, 10-, and 20-mark coins struck in aluminum (and later in magnesium). It is believed that the metal used to make these coins was obtained from downed airplanes. The use of magnesium was unusual; this metal is rarely used for coinage. When shredded or powdered it burns with an intense white flame.

The winters of 1941 through 1943 were harsh for ghetto inhabitants. Coal and wood were rationed, and there was never enough to drive away frostbite, let alone cook food. Without a fire, much of the rations, especially potatoes, could not be eaten. In desperation, the prisoners burned fences, small buildings, and anything available—even the magnesium coins were burned in an effort to stay alive. As a result, these pieces are much scarcer than their aluminum counterparts.

Examples of the Lodz Ghetto tokens are well known to coin collectors, but mostly forgotten by others. The world might be a better place if everyone owned one of these coins and carried it as a reminder of man's inhumanity to man, and the futility of war and aggression.

Magnesium is rarely used for coinage. When shredded or powdered, it burns with an intense white flame.

Five-mark and 10-mark aluminum tokens of the Lodz Ghetto are generally available in Very Fine to Extremely Fine condition for less than $100 each. The 20-mark coins are much scarcer and worth $250. Pieces struck in magnesium are valued only slightly higher, but seem to be much scarcer.

1.96x actual size

THOMAS JEFFERSON · ARCHITECT OF DEMOCRACY
IN GOD WE TRUST
1743
UNITED STATES ASSAYER
UNITED STATES OF AMERICA
887 THOUS
FIFTY DOLLS
1852

CHAPTER 10

Money in America

A Declaration of Independence

Massachusetts. Silver Pine Tree Shilling. 1652

Money in America has changed significantly since the days when tobacco, corn, and foreign coins were the primary media of exchange. The early English settlers bartered for nearly everything, and "country pay" (homegrown produce) was used for most transactions. Three hundred years ago, barter was so prevalent that a man could import a wife from England by paying the shipping cost with 50 pounds of tobacco. In rare instances when foreign currency was received in trade, the colonists were expected to return the coins to England to pay for imported goods and taxes. Despite this serious lack of coins or paper money for local trade, it was not until 1652 that any attempt was made to coin money in the British American colonies.

Many numismatists feel this experiment marked the beginning of a breakaway from the homeland. . . .

Trade with the natives was always carried out by use of barter items. One of the most desirable commodities was a type of shell-beads known as *wampum*. Strings and belts made from the beads had a ceremonial and decorative value to the natives, which the settlers mistook to be a form of money. In 1637 the General Court of Massachusetts ordered that white wampum beads should pass at the rate of six for the penny, and "black" (actually blue) should pass at three for a penny. The beads were made from quahog clam shells that were cut into half-inch tubes and drilled with a lengthwise hole so that they could be sewn together in strings. The shells are mostly white in color, but have an inner strip of dark purple that was scarcer and thus more valuable. Fathom-long strings of wampum were the preferred form of trade item. In time, so much local trade was carried out with wampum that glass and bone imitation beads were imported from Europe as a substitute for the labor-intensive shell beads made locally.

The legendary purchase of Manhattan for trinkets was undoubtedly carried out with trade items, beads, and with belts of wampum that documented the transaction. When woven into belts, wampum traditionally served as a remembrance of special events and agreements, in a society that had no written language.

The first coins struck in British colonial America for local use were small silver pieces made by the Massachusetts Bay Colony. Although necessary because of the dearth of circulating coins, the venture was taken with great apprehension because of fear that the English government would react in a hostile way to the bold Americans. The right of coinage, after all, was a royal prerogative, and not something to be taken lightly. Another compelling motive of the English was their desire to keep the colonies in a state of need, so that American products had to be exported to the mother country in exchange for necessities that could only be imported from England. It was this form of mercantilism that made English trade so successful in the 17th century, and something they did not want to disrupt.

2.14x actual size

By 1652 the emboldened Americans were aware of the troubled situation in England, wherein Oliver Cromwell had taken over the throne. It seemed like a perfect time to exert their wish for independence, and make an attempt to locally produce at least a limited amount of coinage to help serve their needs. The first of these coins were crude simple pieces made in 1652. The design was only the stamped initials NE (for "New England") on one side, and the denomination XII, VI, or III on the other (to indicate 12, 6, or 3 pence). The largest of these was known as a shilling, and was roughly equivalent to the Spanish 2 reales, or two bits.

Massachusetts coinage continued for the next 30 years, but the design was refined by adding various styles of trees and appropriate wording. The original date 1652 was continued, probably to avoid conflict with English law, and partially out of tradition. The most famous of the "tree" coins are of the Pine Tree design, which nearly everyone finds the most attractive. Many numismatists feel this experiment in autonomous coinage marked the beginning of a breakaway from the homeland, and was in effect the very first Declaration of Independence for America.

The famous Pine Tree shillings are some of the most popular of the Massachusetts silver coins, especially those struck on large-size planchets. Values range from about $2,000 in Fine condition, to more than $8,000 in Extremely Fine. An average Very Fine piece, with few distracting marks, would be worth about $4,000. Other denominations and different tree designs are valued according to their scarcity.

Tobacco served as currency in 17th-century Virginia and was traded for supplies from England. Native-made wampum beads were used throughout New England as a valuable trade item. It consisted of small beads made from a quahog clam shell.

1652 Oak Tree shilling. (Actual size)

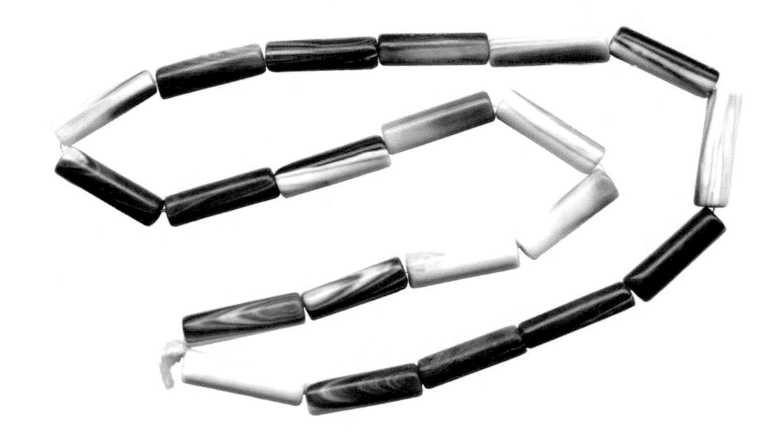

Coins of Necessity

NEW YORK. LIGHTWEIGHT COUNTERFEIT COPPER. 1772

The shortage of copper coins at the end of the 18th century was even more widespread in America than in England. The few coppers that found their way to this side of the ocean were mostly lightweight counterfeit halfpence that had been rejected in the homeland where they were made. Even so, the need for small change made them useful, and any small copper coin of any kind was thankfully taken out of necessity. In many cases they were simply recognized as "coppers," with little regard for the actual or purported denomination.

Lightweight counterfeit copper. (Actual size)

The widespread use of English copper coins, including the ubiquitous lightweight counterfeits, soon inspired crafty Americans to try making their own counterfeit versions of the king's money. The first were made simply by casting crude copies in molds made from impressions of genuine coins. Metal was easily obtained by melting other coins and adding scrap metal or brass to extend the quantity. The size, weight, and quality or these early American counterfeits was below even that of the English versions, but that did not prevent them from circulating.

In time, counterfeit coins became so widely accepted in New England that Yankee ingenuity stepped in. A factory was set up to mass produce the spurious coins, which soon become known as "hardware." James Atlee was the principal operator in a partnership that conducted its clandestine business in Newburgh, New York. Atlee was an engraver by trade and able to produce well-made dies. Their mint was located on land owned by Captain Thomas Machin, known as Machin's Mills. Similar operations were carried out in New York City by John Bailey and Ephraim Brasher, and probably by others who have never been identified. Legend holds that minters who produced these counterfeits wore frightening masks to scare away any who might see them at work.

Designs used on the American-made imitations of lightweight British counterfeits were essentially the same as those on genuine British coins. The obverse had the bust of the king of Britain (either George II or George III), and the reverse featured the seated figure of Britannia. The coins were purposely made to look old, and dates from 1747 to 1784 were often used to disguise them. (Those made by Atlee and dated 1787 or 1788 were likely actually produced in those years.)

Business was successful enough that both New York operations later petitioned other states to obtain coinage rights to make authorized coins, and they did indeed make many of the genuine coins that saw service in this country prior to the opening of the United States Mint. Most of the counterfeiting activities stopped in 1790 when the critical coin shortage ended, and all were driven out of business by 1793, when the first United States coppers were produced.

Machin's Mills coppers are extremely popular for their role in early American commerce. A Very Fine piece, at $800, is considered a high grade, as most are not much better than Good, and are worth about $75.

1.85x actual size

An American Original

Vermont. Landscape Copper. 1786

The Articles of Confederation, adopted March 1, 1781, gave Congress power to regulate the kind of coins made by itself or by the individual states. Each state had the right to coin money, but few exercised that option. Connecticut and New Jersey were the first to experiment with copper coinage, and later Vermont, which did not become a state until 1791, also began production. All three eventually turned part of their coinage operations over to private contractors who earlier had been in the counterfeiting business.

New York never did officially sanction any state coins of its own, but private minters did make coins ostensibly for local use there. Massachusetts was the first state to use the denominations CENT and HALF CENT on its coins (issued in 1787 and 1788), but stopped production when the cost exceeded the face value. All other state coins were similar in size to the familiar British halfpence, but bore no indication of value, and were simply referred to as "coppers."

The coins of Connecticut were purposely designed to imitate the well-known halfpence pieces of Britain that were widely used throughout New England at that time. The bust on the obverse was easily recognized as George II, even though the Latin inscription said "By the Authority of Connecticut." On the reverse a seated figure, looking very much like Britannia, was transformed into Lady Liberty. The coins of Massachusetts showing an American Indian and an eagle, and those of New Jersey, with a plow and shield, are American originals. The legend E PLURIBUS UNUM was innovative and is still being used on all United States coins.

Many collectors think that the unique design on the early coins of Vermont is the most original representation of post-colonial America. On the obverse is a mountain range (the Green Mountains from which Vermont gets its name) and a plow sitting in a field, representing its pastoral beauty. The reverse of the Vermont coppers made from 1785 to 1786 shows a glory of 13 stars with the legend QUATRA DECIMA STELLA ("The Fourteenth Star"), expressing its firm desire to become the 14th state. Sadly, Vermonters did not get their wish until 1791, after the last of their coins were issued.

The "landscape" or "plow" coins of Vermont were made only in 1785 and 1786 because of limited facilities and ability. In 1786 New York minters contracted with the Vermont state government to produce coins for them. The new production did not look like the original coins but resembled the old English coins that were still in circulation. Bust-type coins of Vermont were made from 1786 to 1788, and after 1787 many of the pieces were produced by the clandestine Machin's Mills mint, either on contract or as hastily made counterfeits.

Connecticut state copper, 1787. Such copper coins were all dated from 1785 to 1788, but not necessarily made in those years. (Actual size)

> Vermont landscape coppers in Very Good condition sell for $500 to $600; Very Fine coins are worth more than $2,000. It is unusual to find any that are fully struck on unblemished planchets.

2.22x actual size

A Small Beginning

UNITED STATES OF AMERICA. COPPER FUGIO CENT. 1787

The first federally authorized United States coin was a small copper piece about the size of a modern quarter dollar. It was intended to replace the many different state and foreign coins that were in circulation in 1787, and to bring some stability to their value. The issue was approved by an act of the Continental Congress, and while the denomination is considered a cent, that word does not appear on any of the coins.

It is believed that the design on these coins was inspired by Benjamin Franklin.

It is believed that the design on these coins was inspired by Benjamin Franklin. The central motif is a sundial with a radiate sun above. On the left is the Latin word FUGIO, for "I Flee," and below is MIND YOUR BUSINESS, which should be interpreted to mean, "Time flies so tend to your work." The date 1787 is at the right, and on the reverse is a chain of 13 links around an inner circle inscribed UNITED STATES and WE ARE ONE.

As attractive and useful as these early coins were, they were never a smashing success. Pieces were coined in New Haven, Connecticut, and in New York, but the minters never fulfilled their contract and the function ended without continuation. The limited number of coins that did get into circulation saw extensive use, and they are avidly collected today as mementos of our first coinage.

These coins also brought with them one of the first major scandals involving a government contract. The coins were commissioned to be made by James Jarvis in his home city of New Haven. They were to be of a standard weight and size as mandated by Congress in 1786. The dies for the new coins were made by Abel Buell, but coinage took place not only in that city but also in Newburgh, New York. The design was an adaptation of one formerly used on the Continental Congress experimental pieces made in 1776.

Jarvis, who held the contract to make the coins, placed the operation under the supervision of his father-in-law, Samuel Broome, while he went to Europe to purchase a supply of copper to augment what had been provided by the government. In running the mint, Broome not only produced the Fugio cents, but also continued to make Connecticut coppers by drawing from the government copper. In an effort to hide the embezzling, Broome made his coins slightly under legal weight, and then later fled the country without ever paying the government for any of its copper. Congress voided the Jarvis contract, but the minting did not end there because the dies and equipment were eventually sold to the counterfeiters at Machin's Mills in Newburgh, where more of the lightweight pieces were coined.

A more auspicious start for United States coins began with President George Washington's enthusiasm for coinage to be produced at an official mint. To that end, he selected a suitable building site in Philadelphia and appointed David Rittenhouse as the first Mint

2.22x actual size

director. The president was anxious to have coins as soon as possible and commissioned a neighbor, John Harper, to make a few pieces for his early approval. A small denomination, the half disme, was chosen for these first pieces, and dies engraved with the image of Liberty (some say Martha Washington) on the obverse, and an American eagle on the reverse. It is commonly believed that the president resisted having his portrait used on any American coin because he wanted to break with the old tradition of monarchs, who insisted on that right of sovereignty. The legend on the obverse of these coins reads LIB(erty).PAR(ent).OF SCIENCE & INDUSTRY. The reverse shows a rather awkward-looking eagle with wings outstretched. The denomination is rendered as HALF DISME. Why the French spelling of *dime* was used remains a mystery, but the pronunciation was probably similar to "dime" and the odd spelling was never again used on U.S. coins.

The president in his 1792 address to Congress made mention of the new coins: "There has also been a small beginning in the coinage of half dismes; the want of small coins in circulation calling first attention to them." Approximately 1,500 of the coins were made, and many of them apparently went to President Washington for his personal use. This would have been appropriate because the coins are known to have been made from silver that came from the president's melted household utensils. Today fewer than 250 specimens of this early experimental coinage remain in collectors' hands. Some consider the pieces to be patterns, or trials, while others believe these are the first official United States coins.

1792 half disme. (5x actual size)

The coins were made from silver that came from George Washington's melted household utensils.

Fugio cents in Fine grade sell for $250. Very Fine coins are priced at $600. Many Uncirculated coins still exist and sell at about $2,000. Very Fine examples of the half disme are generally priced at $60,000 or above.

America's Obsolete Coins

UNITED STATES OF AMERICA. COPPER HALF CENT. 1795

The first truly American coin was a half-cent piece made in 1793 at the fledgling mint in Philadelphia, on a hand-operated screw press. Only 35,334 were produced, but it was the beginning of an effort to supply the nation with much-needed small change. Half cents were coined from 1793 to 1857, but not in every year. For some reason they were never as popular, nor as necessary, as their companion large cents made in all but one year during the same period. Production of the half cent ended in 1857 after the cost of copper outweighed its face value. Around that time the large cent was reduced in size and changed to a different composition.

Copper-nickel three-cent piece, 1865. Three-cent coins were made of silver from 1851 to 1873, and of copper-nickel from 1865 to 1889. (1.5x actual size)

It is difficult to determine if the odd half-cent denomination was ever needed. In 1854, Mint Director A. Loudon Snowden said that he considered it useless, and "People will not take the trouble to make a cent with two pieces of money." Its purchasing power must have been about the same as our quarter dollar, the most popular coin in circulation today. Half cents should have been a welcome substitute for the colonial coppers that were still in use until 1857, but even that did not seem to enhance their acceptance. The lowest denomination ever produced by the United States simply never caught on.

Half cents were not the only unusual denomination to come and go in the history of United States coinage. From 1864 to 1872, two-cent coins were produced in an effort to provide additional small change, but these too ended in failure because the public did not accept them. Another attempt at providing convenience was the ill-fated three-cent coin. No one has conclusively determined why such a denomination was wanted; apparently the coins never were really needed, as their limited mintage and low circulation would confirm.

The next Mint calamity was a 20-cent coin so close in size and appearance to the quarter that it caused a public uproar and had to be discontinued after only two years of production. Its design is very much like that of the trade dollar of 1873 to 1883, which also ended in failure even though it contained a bit more silver than a regular dollar coin of the same era.

Gold coins also had their share of unusual denominations. The gold dollar was so small (13 mm) that it was easily lost, and it rarely circulated at a time when silver dollars were all the rage. The quarter eagle ($2.50) gold pieces were an unusual non-decimal denomination, but apparently very popular because they were made from 1796 to 1929. They do, however, raise questions about the need for a $3 coin, a $4 coin, and a $5 coin at the same time, all of which were proposed or tried, with only the $5 coin surviving the test of time.

Examples of all these odd-denomination coins are readily available, except for the $4 gold coins that never went beyond the experimental stage. Any one or all will make a splendid addition to a collection of United States coins.

2.61x actual size

A Wartime Necessity

United States of America. Bronze Civil War Token. Circa 1863

Turmoil caused by the Civil War brought about a shortage of federal coins because of the government's inability to keep up with needed production, and man's age-old habit of hoarding money during times of crisis. Silver and gold coins were traded at a premium over paper money or promissory notes and small change became almost non-existent. The problem, and the final solution, was an oft-repeated story. It fell to merchants and tradesmen to remedy the situation by issuing their own emergency money to carry on business.

At the outset of the war in 1861, several merchants began issuing advertising pieces in the shape and size of regular United States cents. These usually contained the name and address of an individual or business and sometimes a patriotic or political sentiment. While the war continued and escalated, many more establishments began making their own versions of tokens, both as a convenience to trade, and because they were profitable and good advertising. Private mints that manufactured the tokens also began making and selling them in quantity at prices less than 1¢ each. The arrangement was profitable for everyone, helped to ease the coin shortage, and spread patriotism through messages on the tokens.

An estimated 50 million or more Civil War tokens were issued from 1861 through 1864. They are generally divided into two groups: tradesmen's tokens, and anonymously issued pieces with political or patriotic themes. All of them were made by, and for use in, the Northern states, and there are no Confederate issues of these tokens.

The legal status of Civil War tokens was uncertain and a subject of debate at the time they were in use. Director of the Mint James Pollock believed they were illegal, yet there was no law prohibiting the issue of private tokens or coins not in imitation of United States coins. Because of the controversy, most of the tokens had no indication of a denomination on them. Some were inscribed NOT ONE CENT, with the word NOT in very small letters, and ONE CENT much larger.

In an effort to prevent confusion and misunderstanding, and to preserve the U.S. Mint's manufacturing prerogative, a law was passed on April 22, 1864, prohibiting the issue of any one- or two-cent coins, tokens, or devices for use as money. On June 8, 1864, another law was passed that abolished private coinage of every kind, and the era of Civil War tokens ended. Fortunately for everyone, the government Mint was able to satisfy commercial needs by then, and there was no longer any need for a private solution to the problem.

Civil War tokens were normally made in copper or bronze, although pieces are known in other metals. Common patriotic and merchant tokens are worth about $15 in Very Fine, and $40 in Uncirculated. Rare varieties, and those in unusual metals, are valued much higher.

Patriotic Civil War token, 1863. At least 10,000 different designs and varieties have been recorded, and all are avidly sought by collectors. (1.5x actual size)

3.16x actual size

The Gold Rush

United States Assay Office. $50 Gold. 1852

Gold was discovered in California in 1848, and soon a rush was on for people from all over the country to move there in search of the precious metal. The relatively new state was not prepared for such an influx, and commerce suffered from a lack of convenient money for transactions. The only United States mints were located in the eastern part of the country, and transport of needed coins to the West Coast was slow and costly. It was an exasperating situation: the area was flowing with gold, but there was no convenient means of converting it to coined or spendable money.

The large gold coins soon became known as "slugs," it is said because they could be used as an efficient weapon against any would-be robber.

Miners with gold to spend often carried their fine-grained dust in a pouch, and paid for items with whatever could be held between a thumb and finger, called a "pinch." This unruly type of transaction engendered many abuses, and miners sought better ways to protect the value of their newfound wealth. To remedy the situation a number of private companies set up assaying, refining, and coinage operations. At the time there was nothing illegal about making private coins as long as they were of proper weight and value.

The first and most important of the California private minters was the firm of Moffat and Co., which began operations in 1849. The coins they made were of very high quality and accepted everywhere. The assay office they ran was semi-official, and became the forerunner of the United States Mint in San Francisco. Five- and ten-dollar gold coins were made in 1849 and 1850 using designs similar to regular U.S. issues. In 1851 Augustus Humbert, a New York watchcase maker, was appointed United States Assayer, and was commissioned to make dies for a $50 gold piece that was officially termed an *ingot*. These were accepted as legal tender on par with standard U.S. gold coins, but were remarkably different in shape and design. On the obverse is an eagle with outstretched wings. The reverse contains a lathe-pattern design similiar to that used on many contemporary watchcases.

The large $50 coins were heavy, octagonal in shape, and much larger than any other American coin. They soon became known as "slugs," it is said because they could be used as an efficient weapon against any would-be robber. The $50 coins were at first gratefully received by Californians, as they needed a medium that would be accepted by the Custom House (where gold dust and private gold coins were refused). The denomination was, however, too large for ordinary transactions, and a 3% commission was usually charged for conversion into coins of lesser value.

In time many other private companies produced numerous gold coins to facilitate transportation and use of the precious metal. All are scarce and valuable today, and considered to be some of the choicest of all numismatic treasures.

$50 gold pieces are among the most popular and desirable of all privately issued gold coins. Prices begin around $10,000 for Fine specimens, and $50,000 for Uncirculated.

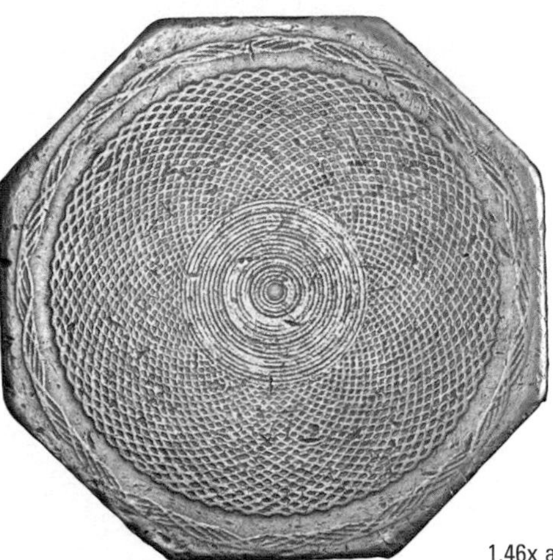

1.46x actual size

Monuments of History

United States. Oregon Trail Commemorative. Half Dollar. 1938

The United States was a latecomer in issuing commemorative coins. The custom of making special coins to honor people, places, and events began in ancient times, and later spread around the world. The first U.S. commemoratives were minted in 1892 to memorialize the voyages of Christopher Columbus and his "discovery" of the New World. Since that time special coins have been made intermittently from 1900 to 1954, and each year from 1982 to the present.

Commemorative coins are exceptional in that they are rarely seen in normal circulation. Most of the hundreds of kinds that have been made in this country over the past 100 years were limited in quantity and only sold as souvenirs or to collectors. Collecting commemorative coins was once the exclusive domain of numismatists, but since the advent of the 50 State Quarters® program and Presidential dollars, and extensive advertising by the U.S. Mint, they have become increasingly more popular. The new wave of interest has also brought attention to many of the older commemoratives that were hitherto unknown to most Americans. It has become an exciting challenge to learn more about the history and artistry of the country through its numismatic heritage.

It was once fashionable to collect one of each different commemorative issue. Most of the early coins were of the half-dollar denomination, and issued at a cost of three or four times face value. Now the early "classic" designs are valued at $100 and up for any of the 142 different pieces that were made prior to the series being interrupted in 1954. When commemorative coinage was resumed in 1982, a new generation of collectors took up the challenge of saving each new issue, but few attempt to assemble full sets of the older pieces because of price considerations. Instead, the trend today is to collect coins of the best possible condition, and concentrate on basic type coins or those of special themes.

Beauty, history, famous people, eagles, animals, and even some people that should never have been depicted on these coins, are all topics that appeal to collectors of the wonderful world of commemoratives. They are coins like none others in United States numismatics, and hold something of interest to everyone. There are no absolute favorites among the hundreds of options available for anyone who wants to own a typical example. Some are noteworthy for their aesthetic appeal, others for their unusual designs that range from poor to extraordinarily beautiful.

A personal favorite, and one that appeals to many others, is the work of the famous husband-and-wife team of James and Laura Fraser. They produced the masterful Oregon Trail Memorial commemoratives that were minted from 1926 through 1939. The obverse of these half dollars shows a covered wagon headed west, and the reverse depicts a Native American superimposed on a map of the United States.

Oregon Trail Memorial coins are generally available at prices from $125 for About Uncirculated, to $175 for MS-63, and $300 for MS-65.

It has become an exciting challenge to learn more about the history and artistry of the country through its numismatic heritage.

2x actual size

The Indian Head Cent

United States of America. Bronze Cent. 1904

James B. Longacre, the designer of the Indian Head cent, would be proud that his artistry has survived the test of time for nearly 150 years. . . .

There was a time when collecting Indian Head cents was the most popular numismatic activity in America. Nearly everyone entered the hobby by trying to put together a date set of Indians, and because most could be found in circulation, or in the family "cookie jar," it was easy to form a nice collection. A beginning collector simply had to keep looking for the best specimens that could be found, or occasionally spend a few dollars to purchase something that was scarce or in high-grade condition.

By 1930 Indian Head cents, which had been coined from 1859 through 1909, were pretty much replaced by Lincoln cents; few of the old coins were still in circulation. They were easy enough to come by because they were the coins that were tossed into a drawer and saved for a rainy day. Very few people were aware that some of the dates were scarcer than others, but anyone who tried to put together a date set soon became aware that 1877 was hard to find. It was a coin with a premium on it, like the 1908-S and 1909-S (San Francisco Mint) cents that were rarely seen outside of the Western states.

Coin collecting became a popular hobby in the 1940s, and a new generation of beginning collectors rushed to fill their "penny boards" with whatever coins they could still find in change. At that time it was not uncommon to find Buffalo nickels, Barber coins, Indian Head cents, and occasionally a Liberty Seated silver piece. Individual prices for Indian Head cents began to firm up after World War II, when collecting began to take off. Common-date cents were worth 2¢ to 3¢ each, while a rarity like 1877 sold for $10 to $15. Anyone ambitious enough to put together an Uncirculated set had to pay around $2 each for most dates, and $3 to $4 each for Proofs.

The passion for collecting Indian Head cents continued into the 1960s, but by then prices were much higher, and choice coins were getting hard to find. Many of the old blazing-red pieces were beginning to fade or turn brown. Over time, collector interest also began to fade and swing to Lincoln cents. Then, for several decades Indian Head cents went out of favor with the masses. All that changed in the mid-1990s when there was a resurgence of interest in the old coppers. As collector demand increased, prices escalated and the race was on to form sets in the best possible condition while such pieces were still available. Their popularity has continued to increase, but at higher price levels, and with a new appreciation for these classic coins.

James B. Longacre, the designer of the Indian Head cent, would be proud that his artistry has survived the test of time for nearly 150 years, and has become a favorite collectible item for millions of hobbyists. It is truly an American classic.

Many dates of the Indian Head cents are equally common and worth similar prices of about $2.50 for Fine, to $30 for basic Uncirculated. Superior pieces, and rare dates, bring prices up to $1,000 or more.

3.16x actual size

Mr. Morgan's Dollars

United States of America. Silver Dollar. 1903-O

Prior to 1873, the United States was on a bimetallic money system. The government coined all the bullion brought to the Treasury on a silver-to-gold ratio of 15 to 1. This often led to the hoarding of gold because of its higher intrinsic value. In 1873 the price of silver rose to $1.30 per ounce, exceeding the face value of a silver dollar, so coinage was halted and not resumed until 1878. After new mines opened in Nevada and Colorado in 1874, the price of silver began to fall to its previous level, and proponents of "free silver" demanded a return to silver coinage at the rate of 16 to 1.

On February 28, 1878, Congress passed the Bland-Allison act, requiring the Treasury to purchase at market price two to four million dollars' worth of silver each month and coin it into silver dollars. Suggestions for new designs were made by Mint engravers; the one selected was proposed by George T. Morgan.

Mint officials seemed more than glad to replace the old Liberty Seated design with something more contemporary, as they had received many complaints about the outdated motif. Morgan had been hired in 1876 as a "special engraver," and was well suited to the task of redesigning the dollar. He had formerly worked for the British Royal Mint in London where he was a pupil of master engraver William Wyon. Throughout 1876, 1877, and 1878, competition raged among Morgan and the other skilled Mint engravers for acceptance of their dollar designs. Models by Mint engravers Anthony Paquet and William Barber were some of the most artistic ever considered, but Morgan's rather stiff head of Miss Liberty, and his eagle with unnaturally raised wings, won the Mint's approval. Why Morgan chose the strange-looking eagle with splayed wings is anybody's guess, but he was proud of his design, and signed the coins with his initial M on the truncation of Liberty's neck and on the reverse on the left bow of the wreath.

Reaction from the public to the new design was warm and accepting. It was a welcome change from the old Liberty Seated pieces that had been in use since 1837, and in keeping with the styles of the day. Throughout their minting, from 1878 to 1921, to today, Morgan silver dollars have been an icon of the mighty American dollar, and a well-respected part of the numismatic scene. From earliest times, collectors have attempted to form full sets of these coins from each date and each of the five mints that made them. In recent times, minor die varieties have received additional attention, and collectors now vie to find pieces in the finest-known level of condition.

Fortunately for collectors, millions of Morgan dollars have survived because of long-term storage in Treasury vaults. It is easy to locate examples of many dates in Uncirculated condition; however, some dates and mintmarks are extremely rare in high grade. The most common type coins are priced from about $15 in Very Good to $40 in MS-63 Uncirculated.

Why Morgan chose the strange-looking eagle with splayed wings is anybody's guess, but he was proud of his design. . . .

1.58x actual size

The Most Famous Lincoln Cent

United States of America. Bronze Cent. 1909-S VDB

Many old-time collectors say they began their interest in coins by attempting to put together a set of Lincoln cents by date and mint. In the 1930s and 1940s it was possible to assemble such sets from coins found in circulation. All that changed by 1950, as many of the scarcer pieces became valuable and were absorbed by the collections of a lucky few. Since that time Lincoln cents have gone through many cycles of popularity and near-obscurity. Through it all there has always been a corps of collectors who long to complete their sets. It seems likely that interest in this series is destined to continue for as long as people collect coins.

Closeup of Victor David Brenner's initials.

Collecting interests often follow a familiar lifetime pattern. The urge to save things usually begins about age 8 to 10, and continues on to puberty, when other more compelling concerns take over. Partially completed sets of Lincoln cents and other things are set aside during college and the early years of marriage and raising a family. Later, when finances are more secure, and leisure time not at such a premium, the appeal of collecting returns. It is at that time that people remember how they longed for those missing dates needed to complete their set of Lincoln cents. It is then that many resolve to acquire those elusive coins at any cost.

The single Lincoln cent that sticks in everyone's memory is the 1909-S VDB. It is missing from nearly every set because fewer than half a million pieces were ever minted, and it has always been a high-premium coin. It also has a catchy name, and is so different from all other cents that it is well known even to non-numismatists. As the "key" to every Lincoln cent collection, it is high on every want list, and its value has risen every year since the early 1950s. There is little doubt that the 1909-S VDB Lincoln cent is the most famous, and one of the most desirable, of all American coins.

Some of the appeal of this coin lies in an unusual feature on the reverse: the designer's initials VDB appear at the bottom edge, beneath the wheat stalks. Victor D. Brenner was proud of his design and placed his initials there in what he thought was a tradition. Others, not understanding the artist's motives, forced their removal from the cent, and thus only a few of the first coins minted at Philadelphia in 1909 have the tiny letters. Even fewer pieces of this variety were made at the San Francisco Mint before the practice was halted, making the strange 1909-S VDB coins an instant rarity. The injustice to Brenner was not corrected until 1918, when his initials were restored to the coins in miniscule letters on the truncation of Lincoln's bust.

1909-S VDB Lincoln cents are generally available in all grades, but at ever-increasing premiums. Pieces in Good condition bring more than $500; Fine, $700; and Extremely Fine, $1,000. Uncirculated coins always sell quickly at $1,500 and up depending on their color and overall appearance.

3.16x actual size

The Most Beautiful American Coin

United States Of America. Saint-Gaudens Gold $20. 1907

Everyone has a favorite coin design, and usually a favorite "dream coin." Sometimes the two are the same. The coin that is high on nearly every list is the $20 gold piece designed by Augustus Saint-Gaudens—a coin world famous for its beauty and rare enough to always be something to anticipate. It is a masterpiece that every collector can fantasize about owning, and hope for, until the day comes when one is added to their collection.

Acquiring a specimen of the standard Saint-Gaudens double eagle should not be a problem for any dedicated collector. Coins with this design were issued in many years from 1907 to 1932, and many dates are readily available in high-grade condition. The design has proven to be so popular over the years that it has been repeated on modern United States bullion gold coins, minted from 1982 to date, albeit with some slight modifications to slim down Miss Liberty and make her look more like a 21st-century beauty.

The most cherished of the Saint-Gaudens coins, however, are the incredible first-style pieces that were coined for only a few months in 1907. Those coins were made in such high relief that it took five strokes of the coinage press to bring up the design, and production was so slow that only 11,250 pieces could be made before the effort was halted.

It is likely that none of the high-relief coins would have been made if not for the insistence of President Theodore Roosevelt, who wanted the United States to have the most beautiful coins in the world. His persistence won out, and he did achieve his goal with this coin. It stands far above all other American numismatic items made before, or since, as the ultimate achievement in the coiner's art.

President Roosevelt knew of, and appreciated, the talent of Irish-born New York artisan Augustus Saint-Gaudens, and personally invited him to design coins that he wanted to be "inspired by ancient Greek art and equal to the finest of any other country." He was immediately pleased with the early designs submitted by the artist, and approved of his proposed $10 and $20 coins, with the request that they be minted as quickly as possible. Despite arguments from the Mint that it would be impossible for them to strike coins in such high relief, the order was given to proceed at any cost.

Saint-Gaudens died in August 1907, and shortly thereafter the Mint altered the dies by lowering the relief so that their equipment could strike the coins efficiently. By late 1907 the new version of the double eagle went into production.

The gorgeous "Saints," as they are known, show a standing figure of Liberty inspired by Greek statues on the obverse and a magnificent flying eagle on the reverse.

In 1907 Saint-Gaudens's Indian Head $10 gold coin was also placed in circulation. (Actual size)

High-relief double eagles are typically priced in excess of $10,000 for Extremely Fine, and $15,000 for Uncirculated.

1.76x actual size

UNITED STATES OF AMERICA
HALF DOLLAR
當

RESOURCES FOR COLLECTORS

Milestone Coins

Gallery of Relative Coin Sizes

This gallery illustrates each of the major coin types featured in *Milestone Coins: A Pageant of the World's Most Significant and Popular Money*. The coins are all shown at actual size, to give the reader a sense of their scale relative to each other.

Ionia, electrum 1/12 stater
(pg 8)

Lydia, electrum 1/3 stater
(pg 9)

Lydia, silver siglos
(pg 10)

Aegina, silver turtle stater
(pg 11)

Metapontion, silver nomos
(pg 12)

Athens, silver tetradrachm
(pg 13)

Aspendos, silver stater
(pg 15)

Syracuse, silver dekadrachm
(pg 16)

Macedon, gold stater
(pg 18)

Macedon, silver tetradrachm
(pg 19)

Egypt, silver tetradrachm
(pg 20)

Kyrenaica, silver tetradrachm
(pg 21)

Roman Republic, silver denarius
(pg 24)

Judaea, bronze lepton
(pg 25)

Byblos, silver dishekel
(pg 26)

Syria, silver tetradrachm
(pg 27)

Rome, silver denarius
(pg 28)

Judaea, bronze lepton
(pg 29)

Tyre, silver tetradrachm or shekel
(pg 30)

Syria, silver drachm
(pg 32)

Rome, denarius
(pg 32)

Judaea, silver shekel
(pg 33)

Judaea, silver sela or shekel
(pg 34)

Rome, small bronze
(pg 35)

Rome, bronze aes grave as
(pg 38)

Rome, silver didrachm
(pg 39)

Rome, silver denarius
(pg 40)

Rome, silver denarius
(pg 41)

Rome, silver denarius
(pg 42)

Rome, silver denarius
(pg 44)

Rome, copper as
(pg 46)

Rome, silver denarius
(pg 47)

Rome, silver denarius
(pg 48)

Rome, silver antoninianus
(pg 49)

Byzantine Empire,
bonze 40 nummia
(pg 52)

Byzantine Empire,
gold solidus
(pg 54)

Byzantine Empire,
gold solidus
(pg 56)

Seljuk Turks, bronze folus
(pg 57)

Sicily, bronze trifollaro
(pg 57)

Crusaders, silver gigliato
(pg 58)

France, silver gros tournois
(pg 59)

England, silver obol
(pg 60)

Mongol tribes, billon dirhem
(pg 61)

Axum, gold 1/3 solidus
(pg 62)

Naples, silver carlino
(pg 64)

Merovingian Kingdom,
gold tremissis
(pg 65)

Turkoman Syria,
bronze dirham
(pg 68)

Turkoman Syria,
bronze dirham
(pg 69)

Arab-Byzantine, bronze fals
(pg 70)

Jerusalem, gold bezant
(pg 70)

Seljuks of Rum, silver dirhem
(pg 71)

Mamluk, bronze fals
(pg 73)

Abbasids, silver dirhem
(pg 74)

Sassanian Kingdom,
silver drachm
(pg 75)

Kashmir, silver rupee
(pg 76)

Egypt, glass token
(pg 77)

Ottoman Empire,
gold double altun
(pg 79)

Early Britain, gold stater
(pg 82)

Roman Britain, sestertius
(pg 83)

Anglo-Saxon Britain,
silver penny
(pg 84)

Anglo-Saxon Britain,
silver penny
(pg 85)

England, silver penny
(pg 86)

England, silver penny
(pg 87)

England, silver groat
(pg 88)

England, silver sixpence
(pg 89)

England, silver penny
(pg 91)

England, silver crown
(pg 92)

England, silver half crown
(pg 93)

England, silver half crown
(pg 93)

Spain, gold double excelente
(pg 96)

Spain, copper 4 maravedís
(pg 97)

Mexico, silver 8 reales
(pg 99)

Bolivia, silver 8 reales
(pg 100)

Mexico, silver 8 reales
(pg 101)

Peru, gold doubloon
(pg 102)

Lima, 8 reales
(pg 103)

England/Spain, 8 reales
(pg 105)

Mexico, silver peso
(pg 106)

Mexico, silver peso
(pg 107)

China, spade money
(pg 110)

China, spade money
(pg 110)

China, round copper coin
(pg 112)

China, copper 5,000 ch'ien
(pg 113)

China, copper cash
(pg 114)

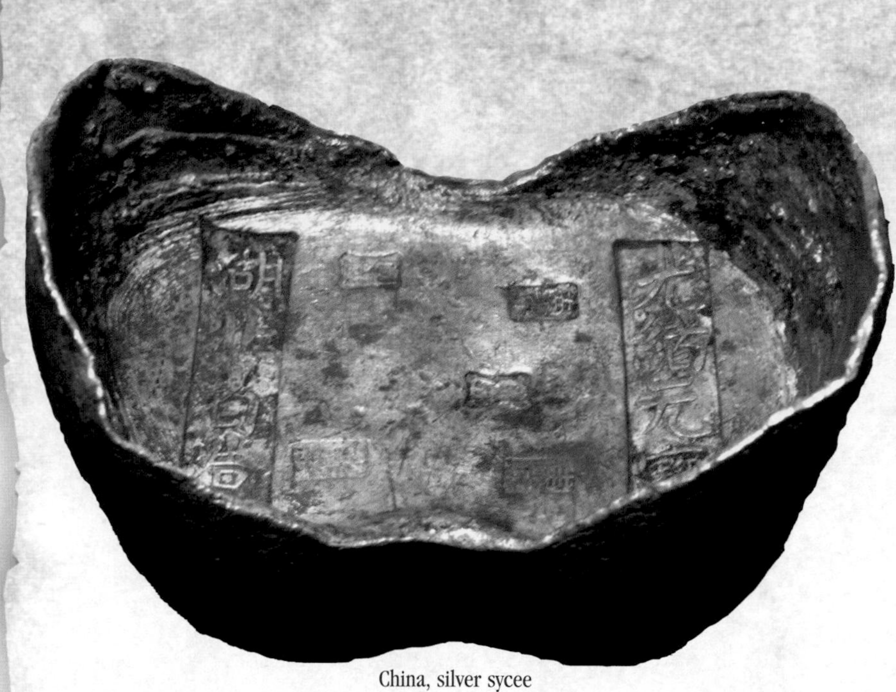
China, silver sycee
(pg 115)

Japan, bronze 100 mon
(pg 116)

China, silver dollar
(pg 117)

China, silver dollar
(pg 118)

China, silver dollar
(pg 119)

Yunnan-Burma, silver tael
(pg 120)

China, silver one-quarter tael
(pg 121)

Netherlands, silver briquet
(pg 124)

Venice, gold ducat
(pg 125)

Bohemia, silver thaler
(pg 126)

Netherlands, paper 5 sols
(pg 128)

Venice, copper gazzetta
(pg 129)

Sweden, copper plate money
(pg 130)

Russia, copper beard tax token
(pg 132)

England, copper token halfpenny
(pg 133)

Britain, copper
"cartwheel" penny
(pg 134)

Austria, silver taler
(pg 135)

Nicaragua, 10 gold pesos
(pg 136)

Poland, Lodz Ghetto,
10 mark
(pg 137)

Massachusetts,
silver Pine Tree shilling
(pg 140)

New York,
counterfeit copper
(pg 142)

Vermont,
Landscape copper
(pg 143)

USA,
copper Fugio cent
(pg 144)

USA,
copper half cent
(pg 146)

USA,
bronze Civil War token
(pg 147)

U.S. Assay Office,
gold $50
(pg 148)

USA,
silver half dollar
(pg 149)

USA,
bronze cent
(pg 150)

USA,
silver dollar
(pg 151)

USA,
bronze cent
(pg 152)

USA,
Saint-Gaudens $20
(pg 153)

Select Bibliography

Album, Stephen. *Marsden's Numismata Orientalia Illustrata.* New York: Attic Books, 1977.

Angell, Norman. *The Story of Money.* Garden City, NY: Garden City Publishing Company, 1929.

Anthony, John. *Collecting Greek Coins.* London: Longman Group, 1983.

Bressett, Kenneth. *Money of the Bible.* 2nd ed. Atlanta, GA: Whitman Publishing, 2007.

Bressett, Kenneth. *Coin Collecting: A Beginner's Guide to the World of Coins.* Atlanta, GA: Whitman Publishing, 2003.

Bressett, Kenneth. *Collectible American Coins.* Lincolnwood, IL: Publications International, 1991.

Bressett, Kenneth. *A Guide Book of English Coins.* Various editions. Racine, WI: Western Publishing, 1962–1982.

Carson, R.A.G. *Coins of the World.* New York and Evanston: Harper & Row, 1962; revised 1970.

Clain-Stefanelli, Elvira and Vladimir. *The Beauty and Lore of Coins.* New York: Riverwood Publishers, 1974.

Doty, Richard G. *The Macmillan Encyclopedic Dictionary of Numismatics.* New York: Macmillan Publishing, 1982.

Forrer, Leonard S. *The Art of Collecting Coins.* London and New York: Citadel Press, 1955.

Goldberg, Ira and Larry, editors. *Money of the World: Coins That Made History.* Atlanta, GA: Whitman Publishing, 2007.

Harris, Robert P. *Pillars & Portraits.* San Jose, CA: Bonanza Press, 1968.

Head, Barclay V. *Historia Numorum. A Manual of Greek Numismatics.* 3rd edition. Oxford, 1911.

Hendin, David. *Guide to Biblical Coins.* 4th edition. New York: Amphora, 2001.

Jenkins, G.K. *Ancient Greek Coins.* New York: G.P. Putnam's Sons, 1972.

Klawans, Zander H., and K.E. Bressett, editor. *Handbook of Ancient Greek & Roman Coins.* New York: Golden Books Publishing Company, 1995.

Kraay, C.M. and Max Hirmer. *Greek Coins.* London: Thames and Hudson, 1966.

Krause, Chester L. and Clifford Mishler. *Standard Catalog of World Coins.* Various editions. Iola, WI: Krause Publications.

Levinson, Robert A. *The Early Dated Coins of Europe,* 1234–1500. New York: Coin and Currency Institute, 2007.

Lindheim, Leon. *Facts & Fictions About Coins.* Cleveland, OH: World Publishing, 1967.

Lobel, Richard. Coincraft's *Standard Catalogue of English & UK Coins,* 1066 to Date. Iola, WI: Krause Publications, 1998.

Opitz, Charles J. *An Ethnographic Study of Traditional Money.* Ocala, FL: First Impressions Printing, 2000.

Porteous, John. *Coins in History.* New York: G.P. Putnam's Sons, 1969.

Porteous, John. *Coins.* London: Octopus Books, 1973.

Price, Martin Jessop. *Coins, An Illustrated Survey 650 BC to the Present Day.* London: British Museum Publications, 1980.

Rawlings, Gertrude B. *Coins and How to Know Them.* London: Methuen & Co., 1908.

Sayles, Wayne G. *Ancient Coin Collecting II.* Iola, WI: Krause Publications, 1997.

Spink. *Coins of England and the United Kingdom.* London: Various modern editions.

Spengler, William F. and Wayne G. Sayles. *Turkoman Figural Bronze Coins and Their Iconography.* Vol. 1, 1992; Vol. 2, 1996. Lodi, WI: Clio's Cabinet.

Suetonius. *The Lives of the Twelve Caesars.* Various English translation and publications.

Sutherland, C.H.V. *Roman Coins.* New York: G.P. Putnam's Sons, 1974.

Whitting, P.D. *Byzantine Coins.* New York: G.P. Putnam's Sons, 1973.

Vaccaro, Francesco. "Le Monete di Aksum." *Italia Numismatica* 1967.

Vermeule, Cornelius. *Numismatic Art in America: Aesthetics of the United States Coinage,* 2nd ed. Atlanta, GA: Whitman Publishing, 2007.

Yeoman, R.S., and Kenneth Bressett. *A Guide Book of United States Coins.* Atlanta, GA.: Whitman Publishing, 2007.

Index

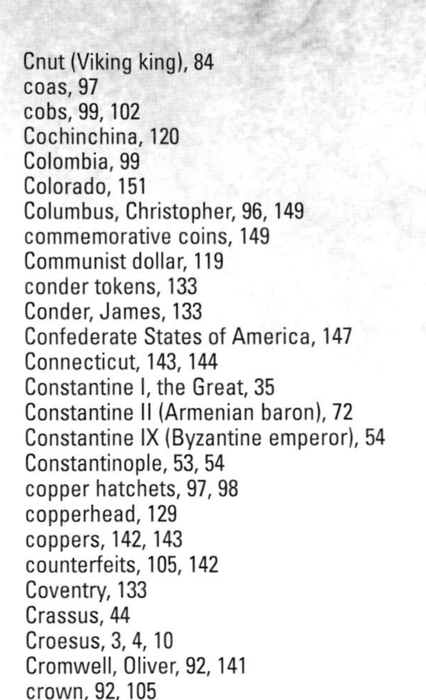

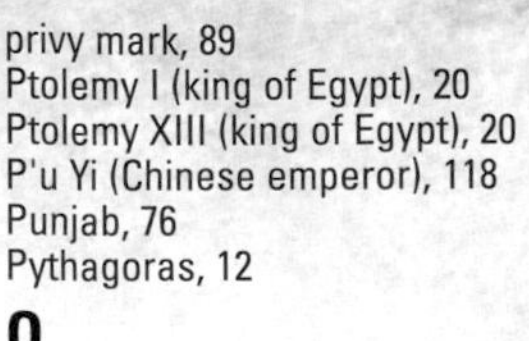